Take &Re

The Acts of
the Apostles

Henry Wansbrough
edited by Adrian Graffy

Published in 2011 by Alive Publishing Ltd.
Graphic House, 124 City Road, Stoke on Trent, ST4 2PH.
Tel: +44 (0) 1782 745600   Fax: +44 (0) 1782 745500
www.alivepublishing.co.uk

©2011 Alive Publishing
British Library Catalogue-in-Publication Data.
A catalogue record for this book is available from the British Library.

ISBN 978-1-906278-12-0

Front cover and page 1: Maesta, upper section: Pentecost, by Duccio.

Contents

Editor's Foreword

One of the features of the Church of today is the rediscovery of the Bible. In the years since the Second Vatican Council this thirst for the Scriptures has become stronger and stronger. The desire for a deeper engagement with the Bible is clear from the enormous popularity of publications such as *Walk with Me* and *Bible Alive*.

Take and Read is designed to assist people in their need to understand the Bible more deeply. The series has been developed as a follow-up to the document *The Gift of Scripture*, which was produced in 2005 by the Bishops of England and Wales, and of Scotland, to mark the 40th anniversary of the Council document on Divine Revelation, *Dei Verbum*.

The story of the conversion of Saint Augustine to the Catholic faith inspired the title of the series. He recounts in his 'Confessions' how he heard a voice calling to him with the words *Tolle, lege* 'Take and Read'. At that moment he picked up the New Testament and read the first chapter his eyes fell upon, from the Letter to the Romans. His conversion was assured.

These books are a major new resource for prayerful reading of the Scriptures both for groups and for individuals. Passages from the Scriptures are accompanied by commentary, quotations from the Fathers and from Church documents, Christian art and inspiring photographs, as well as suggestions for prayer and reflection.

It is a great pleasure to acknowledge the work of those who helped develop this series. Representatives from dioceses throughout Britain worked on the preparatory stages. Particular thanks should go to Anne White, Anne Dixon and Sister Vicky Hummel. I record my gratitude to the authors who have collaborated with me in working on the series. After the initial books on the four gospels we are now turning our attention to other books of the New Testament. I am particularly grateful for the support of Mike Conway of *Alive Publishing*, who readily agreed to publish the *Take and Read* series.

Take and Read will help you to delve more deeply into the Scriptures, to understand them better, and to pray with the Scriptures. *Take and Read* will assist you in *lectio divina*, that prayerful reading of Scripture which has always been central to the life of the Church.

Fr Adrian Graffy

Introduction to the Acts of the Apostles

The Acts of the Apostles is the story of the early Church. Its programme is given by the Risen Christ just before the Ascension (*Acts 1:8*). The apostles are to witness to Jesus in Jerusalem (chapters 1-7), throughout Judaea and Samaria (chapters 8 to 10), and to the ends of the earth (chapters 11-28). This last is a code-word for Rome, the greatest city in the world at that time. The first two missions are done by all the apostles, under the leadership of Peter, the last by Paul and his team. It is a heroic story of courage and conviction against a background of danger, persecution and the threat of martyrdom. At the same time, the apostles are guided and strengthened at every stage of their operations by the Spirit which Jesus had promised they would receive. Especially it underlines the peace, unity, harmony and prayerfulness of the fledgling Church.

The Acts is really a second volume to Luke's first volume, his gospel. It does not itself tell us who the author was, but the similarities to Luke are unmistakable. It is written for an audience of educated Gentiles, somewhere in the Hellenistic world. It has the same emphases as the gospel, a stress on the need for conversion, on the activity of the Spirit, on the fulfilment of prophecy. Above all, it shows how an originally Jewish movement broke its bonds and won its way in the Gentile world. The instrument for this was, always under the guidance of the Spirit, the tireless and energetic apostle Paul.

The conclusion of the whole double-volume story in Rome is highly significant, for the author has insisted throughout that there is no hostility between Christianity and the Roman rule. Any opposition comes from those Jews who were unwilling to recognise in Christianity the fulfilment of the Jewish hopes. However, as the great Jewish teacher Gamaliel warns the Sanhedrin, if the movement is indeed from God, they will be unable to destroy it (*Acts 5:39*).

Opposite: Ms Hunter 229 f.12v Pentecost, from the 'Hunterian Psalter', English School.

The Coming of the Spirit

Hear the Word of God

Read Acts 2:1-21

When the day of Pentecost had come, they were all together in one place. ² And suddenly from heaven there came a sound like the rush of a violent wind, and it filled the entire house where they were sitting. ³ Divided tongues, as of fire, appeared among them, and a tongue rested on each of them. ⁴ All of them were filled with the Holy Spirit and began to speak in other languages, as the Spirit gave them ability.

⁵ Now there were devout Jews from every nation under heaven living in Jerusalem. ⁶ And at this sound the crowd gathered and was bewildered, because each one heard them speaking in the native language of each. ⁷ Amazed and astonished, they asked, 'Are not all these who are speaking Galileans? ⁸ And how is it that we hear, each of us, in our own native language? ⁹ Parthians, Medes, Elamites, and residents of Mesopotamia, Judea and Cappadocia, Pontus and Asia, ¹⁰ Phrygia and Pamphylia, Egypt and the parts of Libya belonging to Cyrene, and visitors from Rome, both Jews and proselytes, ¹¹ Cretans and Arabs — in our own languages we hear them speaking about God's deeds of power.' ¹² All were amazed and perplexed, saying to one another, 'What does this mean?' ¹³ But others sneered and said, 'They are filled with new wine.'

¹⁴ But Peter, standing with the eleven, raised his voice and addressed them: 'Men of Judea and all who live in Jerusalem, let this be known to you, and listen to what I say. ¹⁵ Indeed, these are not drunk, as you suppose, for it is only nine o'clock in the morning. ¹⁶ No, this is what was spoken through the prophet Joel:

¹⁷ "In the last days it will be, God declares,
>   that I will pour out my Spirit upon all flesh,
>   and your sons and your daughters shall prophesy,
>   and your young men shall see visions,
>   and your old men shall dream dreams.
> ¹⁸ Even upon my slaves, both men and women,
>   in those days I will pour out my Spirit;
>   and they shall prophesy.
> ¹⁹ And I will show portents in the heaven above
>   and signs on the earth below,
>   blood, and fire, and smoky mist.
> ²⁰ The sun shall be turned to darkness
>   and the moon to blood,
>   before the coming of the Lord's great and glorious day.
> ²¹ Then everyone who calls on the name of the Lord shall be saved."'

Understand the Word of God

This session will explore:

- ❖ the coming of the Spirit in the life of the Church
- ❖ the speeches in the Acts of the Apostles
- ❖ the role of Peter
- ❖ the use of Scripture in the early Church

Setting in the Book

The Acts of the Apostles begins with the Ascension of Christ. This was the end of the forty days of preparation, in which the Risen Christ instructed his disciples for their mission. The disciples were told to go back into Jerusalem and await the coming of the Spirit who would guide them in their mission. This scene is that coming, and so it constitutes the birth of the Church.

Without the Spirit the disciples can do nothing. They were huddled in the Upper Room, a depressed, bewildered and scared little group, unsure of themselves and not daring to face the world, certainly not daring to proclaim the Resurrection of Christ. By the Spirit they are suddenly transformed into courageous apostles, proclaiming the message of Christ's Resurrection.

In the long speech which follows, of which you have just read the opening verses, Peter explains the meaning of this coming of the Spirit. It brings to a conclusion the purposes of God with the world, and introduces the final stage of world-history, in which we ourselves still live.

Peter makes use of three biblical texts in his speech. At the end of our passage comes the first of these, the long quotation from the book of the prophet Joel. Acts is the story of the transition of the Good News from the Jews to the Gentiles, and, as the speech continues, Peter will not hesitate to blame the Jews for the crucifixion. However, he also enters a certain plea of excuse by saying 'this man was handed

St John Chrysostom says this about the Acts of the Apostles:

To many people this book, both its content and its author, is so little known that they are not even aware it exists. I have therefore taken this narrative for my subject, both to initiate those who are ignorant and so that such a treasure shall not remain hidden out of sight. For indeed it will profit us no less than the Gospels themselves, so replete is it with Christian wisdom and sound doctrine, especially in what is said concerning the Holy Spirit. (Homilies on the Acts of the Apostles 1)

over to you according to the definite plan and foreknowledge of God' (verse 23).

The argument uses and depends on the Greek version of the Psalm, for the Hebrew has 'to see the pit'. The Hebrew would imply that Jesus did not die, whereas the Greek implies that his body did not corrupt. There are two important consequences of this, first that the speech must have been composed in Greek, and can never actually have been given in Hebrew on the day of Pentecost – at least not as it stands – and secondly that the original Bible of the Church was the Greek version rather than the Hebrew.

The second text which Peter will take up is Psalm 16. He uses it to prove the Resurrection. David is assumed to be the author of the Psalm and to be prophesying about Jesus when he says, 'You will not allow your Holy One to see corruption'.

The third text which Peter will take up in verse 34 will be the great Psalm 110: 'The Lord said to my Lord, sit at my right hand.' This is used frequently in the New Testament to prove the exaltation of the Risen Christ to God's right hand.

At the end of the speech it is reported that 'about three thousand' Jews in Jerusalem are converted (verse 41).

What Kind of Text?

The book of the Acts is the story of the earliest Church, and it is written according to the conventions of short histories at that time. Luke, the author also of the Third Gospel, makes this clear by his introduction, which is typical of the introductions to the many little scientific or historical pamphlets of the time which have survived. There is a dedication to an important person, Theophilus.

Luke is a genius at presenting a theological truth in the form of a memorable story or scene. Think of the scene of the Annunciation to Mary or the Journey to Emmaus! From the other gospels we could never guess that this great public 'launch' of the Church took place on the day of Pentecost. In Matthew chapter 28 the Risen Christ charges the disciples to preach to all nations and blesses them on a mountain in Galilee. In John chapter 20 Christ breathes the Spirit on the disciples in the upper room, giving them power to forgive sin, and so sends them out.

Two of the conventions of histories of the time are worth mentioning here. The first is that the author was meant to entertain as well as to instruct. Luke certainly manages this, for he includes many exciting and amusing incidents, escapes from prison, riots, shipwreck, tense law-court disputes and narrow escapes from death. These were the sort of scenes in which contemporary audiences delighted.

A second convention was the use of speeches to explain the significance of an event. A modern historian will relate an event and then comment on it. The ancient historian puts this comment in the mouth of one of his characters, saying not so much what he actually said on the occasion, as though taken down in shorthand, but what that character would have said or should have said. About a quarter of the book is devoted to these speeches, which in fact give the inspired author's commentary on what is going on.

St Bede, who wrote two books on the Acts, comments:

Theophilus means lover of God or beloved of God. Therefore, anyone who is a lover of God may believe that this work was written for him, because the physician Luke wrote it in order that the reader might find health for his soul. (Commentary on the Acts of the Apostles, 1.1)

The Lord came down to see the city and the tower, which mortals had built. And the Lord said, 'Look, they are one people, and they have all one language; and this is only the beginning of what they will do; nothing that they propose to do will now be impossible for them. Come, let us go down, and confuse their language there, so that they will not understand one another's speech'.
(Genesis 11:5-7)

Another significant feature of Luke's story-telling is also evident on this occasion: he presents the events against their Old Testament background. Often the full significance of the events can be understood only by those who are alert to this background. At the Tower of Babel (*Genesis 11*) the peoples were all divided by being unable to understand one another's languages. At Pentecost they are brought together by the ability of different nations to understand Peter's speech in their own language.

Tower of Babel, by Bruegel.

Commentary: verse by verse reading

The coming of the Spirit

vv.1-3 The ministry of Jesus began with the descent of the Spirit at his baptism. So the ministry of his apostles begins with the descent of the Spirit at Pentecost. This stresses that Christians can do nothing without the help and guidance of the Spirit. Without the Spirit there is no Church. The story brings to mind the story of the descent of the spirit of God on the seventy elders of Israel in the time of Moses (*Numbers 11:24-25*). They were to share his task of guiding the people of God. According to later Jewish interpretation the Spirit came down then also in the form of tongues of fire, and the seventy elders represented the seventy nations of the world.

v.4 Different forms of speaking in tongues seem to be attested in the New Testament. Here the speaking in tongues is speaking in a language which was understood by the hearers in their own languages. Elsewhere in Acts 10:46 and 19:6 it leads to 'prophecy', and it is unclear whether this is intelligible or not. The speaking in tongues described at Corinth by Paul in 1 Corinthians 14 seems to have been an overflowing in prayer which required an interpreter. It is, however, always a manifestation of the presence of the Spirit.

vv.5-13 Pentecost, as its name ('fiftieth') implies, falls on the fiftieth day after Passover. The two feasts signal the beginning and end of the grain harvest. They are two of the three great pilgrimage feasts, when huge numbers of Jews would come up to Jerusalem. The list of peoples is probably based on an ancient astrological list, following the signs of the zodiac. It signifies all the nations of the known world, reversing the disunity and dispersal of Babel.

We read in the Catechism of the Catholic Church:

While water signifies birth and the fruitfulness of life given in the Holy Spirit, fire signifies the transforming energy of the Holy Spirit's actions. The prayer of the prophet Elijah, who 'arose like fire' and whose 'word burnt like a torch', brought down fire from heaven on the sacrifice on Mount Carmel. This event was a 'figure' of the fire of the Holy Spirit, who transforms what he touches. (696)

Acts 10:46 They heard them (Cornelius and his companions) speaking in tongues and extolling God.

Acts 19:6 When Paul had laid his hands on them (the disciples at Ephesus), the Holy Spirit came upon them, and they spoke in tongues and prophesied.

1 Corinthians 14:13-15 Therefore, one who speaks in a tongue should pray for the power to interpret. For if I pray in a tongue, my spirit prays but my mind is unproductive. What should I do then? I will pray with the spirit, but I will pray with the mind also.

Peter's speech

vv.14-15 Peter's speech now proceeds, after the manner of Hellenistic historians, to explain the significance of the event. He does so by reference to the Scriptures, using a technique which is familiar from the Dead Sea Scrolls. The scriptural commentaries there take a text and then apply it to contemporary events, with the formula 'Interpreted, this means'.

In the New Testament the sense of many of the doings of Jesus is understood as fulfilment of the Scriptures, and is even described in terms which make the allusions clear. The many scriptural allusions throughout the Passion Narrative suggest that it was all foretold in the Scriptures.

The position of Peter in the Acts is interesting. He has already taken the lead in chapter 1 in the election of a successor to Judas. For the first fifteen chapters he will be the leading figure in the community. Peter and John are sent to lead the first mission outside Jerusalem, in Samaria (*8:14*). Peter has the vision which abolishes the Jewish food laws for Christians, baptises the first gentiles to be received into the community, and justifies his action before the other leaders (chapters 10-11). At the Council of Jerusalem, narrated in chapter 15, he makes the first and decisive speech. Then suddenly he disappears and is not heard of again, leaving James seemingly in charge of the community at Jerusalem.

vv.16-18 Peter takes three texts to explain the events. First, to explain the outpouring of the Spirit, he quotes Joel 3:1-5. This becomes the proof that the last days have arrived. Throughout this incident all Luke's stress is on universalism: the days when the Jews alone could be considered the Chosen People of God have come to an end, and God's favour is now bestowed on all peoples. Isaiah 2:2 had prophesied that all nations would stream to Jerusalem to draw salvation from the mountain of the Lord, and the descent of the Spirit shows that this has occurred.

In Paul's letter to the Galatians Peter appears again at Antioch, but only to be browbeaten in turn by envoys from James in Jerusalem and by Paul himself (2:11-14). Christian tradition holds that he was martyred at Rome. Peter did not found the Church of Rome, nor was he its first bishop, for the office evolved only later, but Peter sanctified Rome with his blood.

vv. 19-20 The imagery used is apocalyptic. In the later books of the Old Testament such imagery is common to describe the cataclysmic Great Day of the Lord, on which the Lord would suddenly come to fulfil his purposes and right all wrongs. This coming is described in terms of cosmic disaster, in which nature itself will be turned upside down. The imagery becomes more and more lurid in the prophetic tradition. This, rather than any perceivable eclipse of the sun, is of course the meaning of the darkness at noon on the day of the crucifixion, a direct quotation from Amos 8:9, to show that this was the Great Day of the Lord.

Amos 8:9 On that day, says the Lord God, I will make the sun go down at noon, and darken the earth in broad daylight.

V.21 In the Acts Christians are again and again described as those who call on the name of the Lord. In Acts 22:16 Saul is invited by Ananias to be baptised 'calling on his name'. Baptism is in, or into, the name of Jesus. Those who are baptised call on the name of Jesus, and the name of Jesus is called over them. Peter will say in 2:38: 'Repent, and be baptised everyone of you in the name of Jesus Christ.' But of course the Lord is no longer simply the Lord in the Old Testament sense. It is rather the Lord Jesus. The reverence paid to Jesus, this title, and the position he enjoys as Saviour, a title originally given only to the Lord God, all show the earliest belief in the divinity of Jesus.

Tornado devastation.

The Word Lives On

Acts 2:1-11, the coming of the Spirit, provides the first reading for Pentecost in each year of the cycle. The part of Peter's speech we are considering is not given in the lectionary, though verses 22-32, which illustrate the Resurrection from Psalm 16, are read on Easter Monday, and verses 22-28 on the Third Sunday of Easter in Year A. Part of Peter's speech is also a reading for Doctors of the Church during the Easter season, illustrating that the Spirit is the source of all wisdom and understanding.

Tongues of fire are often a feature of Christian iconography. A tongue of fire hovering over the head of a saint shows the saint's wisdom and sanctity, suggesting that his or her whole life is inspired by the Spirit.

The Tomb of the Venerable Bede in Durham Cathedral.

Live the Word of God

Listen again to the reading: Acts 2:1-21

Suggestions for reflection and prayer

The Spirit of the Risen Christ came upon the apostles at Pentecost. The Spirit continues to live on in the Church.

❖ guiding the Pope and the other Bishops in their task of directing and teaching the Church

❖ guiding the great teachers of the Church to understand the mysteries of the faith ever more deeply

❖ inspiring the other ministers of the Church, priests, deacons, ministers of the Word and of the Eucharist, teachers and all who work for Christ, in their daily tasks

❖ enabling me, if I open my heart to the Spirit, to respond with love and care to all those in need whom I can help

The Risen and glorified Christ is present in us through the Spirit.

❖ We are all one in Christ living with Christ's life. When I hurt, injure, neglect or cheat someone else, I am doing this to Christ.

❖ In God's eyes there is no distinction between races, colours, prince and pauper, success or failure – except in how we respond to and live by the Spirit.

❖ We should bring the strength and joy of the Risen Christ to all those around us, to everyone we meet.

We come to know God and the divine purposes by reading and reflecting on the Scriptures. Choose a phrase or two from Peter's speech to inspire you and energise you throughout the day.

In the very giving of the Law and of grace a clear distinction becomes apparent between the Old and the New Testaments. In the Old Testament the people stood afar off; there was fear and no love. They were so afraid that they said to Moses, 'You speak to us, lest the Lord speak to us and we die'. So God came down, as it is written, on Sinai in the form of fire, terrifying the people standing afar off. He wrote the Law with his finger on stone, not by his Spirit on their hearts. In the New Testament when the Holy Spirit came the faithful were gathered together. The Spirit did not frighten them on a mountain but entered the house. (St Bede, Retractations on the Acts of the Apostles, c.2)

The First Christian Community

Hear the Word of God

Read Acts 2:37-3:8

37 Now when they heard this, they were cut to the heart and said to Peter and to the other apostles, 'Brothers, what should we do?' 38 Peter said to them, 'Repent, and be baptized every one of you in the name of Jesus Christ so that your sins may be forgiven; and you will receive the gift of the Holy Spirit. 39 For the promise is for you, for your children, and for all who are far away, everyone whom the Lord our God calls to him.' 40 And he testified with many other arguments and exhorted them, saying, 'Save yourselves from this corrupt generation.' 41 So those who welcomed his message were baptized, and that day about three thousand persons were added.

42 They devoted themselves to the apostles' teaching and fellowship, to the breaking of bread and the prayers. 43 Awe came upon everyone, because many wonders and signs were being done by the apostles. 44 All who believed were together and had all things in common; 45 they would sell their possessions and goods and distribute the proceeds to all, as any had need. 46 Day by day, as they spent much time together in the temple, they broke bread at home and ate their food with glad and generous hearts, 47 praising God and having the goodwill of all the people. And day by day the Lord added to their number those who were being saved.

3:1 One day Peter and John were going up to the temple at the hour of prayer, at three o'clock in the afternoon. 2 And a man lame from birth was being carried in. People would lay him daily at the gate of the temple called the Beautiful Gate so that he could ask for alms from those entering the temple. 3 When he saw Peter and John about to go into the temple, he asked them for alms. 4 Peter looked intently at him, as did John, and said, 'Look at us.' 5 And he fixed his attention on them, expecting to receive something from them. 6 But Peter said, 'I have no silver or gold, but what I have I give you; in the name of Jesus Christ of Nazareth, stand up and walk.' 7 And he took him by the right hand and raised him up; and immediately his feet and ankles were made strong. 8 Jumping up, he stood and began to walk, and he entered the temple with them, walking and leaping and praising God.

Opposite: St Peter Preaching, by Fra Angelico. In this painting, St Mark is portrayed as noting down what Peter says.

Understand the Word of God

This session will explore:

- ❖ the idea of repentance in Acts
- ❖ the origin, meaning and purpose of baptism
- ❖ the life of the first, ideal community in Jerusalem
- ❖ the healings worked by the apostles

Setting in the Book

'Christ' is the Greek form of the Hebrew 'Messiah', meaning 'Anointed One'. The believers were given this name [Christians] because they recognised Jesus as the Anointed One, promised by God. The name is a sort of nickname, and has a slightly pejorative or mocking tone. This gives Christians the proud title of being fools for the sake of Christ.

Peter's speech at Pentecost is the first public announcement of the Good News of Christ's Resurrection, and an explanation of its significance, based on three passages of scripture. Now follows the immediate favourable reaction, as the community of believers begins to be formed. It is not yet correct to call them 'Christians', for it was only at Antioch, in 11:26, that they began to be called 'Christians'.

What Kind of Text?

This passage consists of three different kinds of text. First comes the immediate reaction to Peter's speech of the crowds gathered in Jerusalem for the festival of Pentecost. There follows, in verses 42-47, a summary passage describing the salient features of the young community. This is one of several summaries about the life of the young community, another being 4:32-35. For Luke, Jerusalem is the pivot of the gospel. His gospel begins and ends in Jerusalem, and the second half of the gospel consists of the ominous great journey up to Jerusalem. The meetings with the Risen Christ in Luke occur in and around Jerusalem, and then the Good News begins to spread from there. So it is fitting that a summary description should be given of this first group of believers in the holy city of Jerusalem as the ideal and model community for the Church.

The story of the first miraculous cure worked by Peter, which follows in 3:1-8, is a straightforward miracle story, not unlike the miracle stories of Jesus in the gospels, but it has its own special message, as we shall see.

Stories of miraculous cures occur in other religions apart from Christianity. The shrines of ancient pagan healing-gods are often decorated with the crutches or wax models of limbs or eyes, as testimony from those who attribute their cures to gods such as Aesculapius. Without making any judgment on these claims, we may consider the healings of Jesus as the result of an encounter with the awesome and staggering personality of the man who was divine.

Opposite: The modern city of Antakya in Turkey lies close to the Syrian Antioch.

Commentary: verse by verse reading
The reaction of the crowd

v.37 Those who respond to Peter call him and the other apostles 'brothers' (Greek *adelphoi*). This Christian address is nowadays often translated in the New Testament 'brothers and sisters'. This slightly clumsy formula is perhaps unavoidable if it is to be stressed that in Christ there is 'no longer male and female, for all of you are one in Christ Jesus' (*Galatians 3:28*). 'Siblings' would be a more accurate translation, though intolerably precious and analytical. The point is that Christians form what sociologists call a 'fictive family', a family really united in behaviour and ties, though not united by blood, having come into being by other means.

v.38 'Repent!' is the constant cry from the time of John the Baptist (*Matthew 3:2*) and the beginning of Jesus' message onwards (*Mark 1:15*). In modern parlance 'repentance' tends to mean being sorry for sin, weeping over one's iniquity. A more fitting translation of the concept would be 'Change your ways!' It is not a matter of weeping and lamenting but of decisive action. If we are to adopt the ways of the Kingdom, to live the truth that the time of God's full sovereignty has arrived, then a whole new set of standards has to be adopted.

So, if the hearers are to adopt Jesus as their Lord and Saviour, they must adopt a new way of life and a new set of standards. Without this, baptism is meaningless. Each of the proclamations of Acts ends with this appeal for repentance, and in each it has the same meaning.

Baptism is the normal mode of entry into the community of believers, though we read in Acts 10:44-48 that Cornelius and his household receive the gift of the Spirit before they are baptized. It is impossible to be sure of the origins of this rite.

Acts 3:19 Peter said: 'Repent, therefore, and turn to God so that your sins may be wiped out.'

Acts 10:43 Peter said: 'Everyone who believes in him receives forgiveness of sins through his name.'

Acts 17:30 Paul said: 'God commands all people everywhere to repent.'

The community of Qumran practised ritual washing before the daily meal in expectation of the Messiah. However, the baptism of John the Baptist and Christian baptism are once-for-all events. The rite of baptism may have connections with the entry of proselytes into full membership of the Jewish community, but there is no evidence that proselyte baptism existed so early.

As well as the repentance referred to by Peter and the washing away of sin, Christian baptism also has the positive aspect of commitment to Christ. It is the expression of putting all one's trust in Christ, and without that makes no sense at all. For this reason it is often called 'baptism into Christ' or 'into the name of Christ'. In Acts 19:5 we read: 'they were baptized into the name of the Lord Jesus'. Baptism constitutes entry into Christ.

vv. 39-40 Peter stresses even now, and in the heart of Jerusalem, that salvation in Christ is for both Jew and Gentile. He alludes to Isaiah 57:19, in the final part of the book of Isaiah. This text was written after the return from exile in Babylon, when Judaism was already becoming aware of its mission to bring salvation to the Gentiles. The full text reads: 'Peace, peace to the far and the near, says the Lord.' This passage will be used again to great effect in the Letter to the Ephesians, when hostility between Jews and Gentiles in the Church has been overcome. In Ephesians 2:17-18 we read: 'So Christ came and proclaimed peace to you who were far off and peace to those who were near; for through him both of us have access in one Spirit to the Father.'

v.41 Baptism follows for those who accept Peter's preaching, and 'that day about three thousand persons were added'. At several points in Acts the numerical growth of the Church is stressed.

Jesus calls to conversion. This call is an essential part of the proclamation of the Kingdom. It is by faith in the Gospel and by Baptism that one renounces evil and gains salvation, that is, the forgiveness of all sins and the gift of new life. (Catechism of the Catholic Church 1427)

Acts 2:47 And day by day the Lord added to their number those who were being saved.

Acts 4:4 Many of those who heard the word believed, and they numbered about five thousand.

Acts 5:14 More than ever believers were added to the Lord, great numbers of both men and women.

Acts 6:7 The word of God continued to spread and the number of the disciples increased greatly in Jerusalem.

The life of the community

vv.42-47 Luke now paints a picture of the ideal first community at Jerusalem, showing Christian community as it should be. The new Christians were faithful 'to the apostles' teaching'. The teaching (Greek *didache*) should be distinguished from the initial preaching (Greek *kerygma*). It was the task of the apostles to bear witness to Christ. The apostles were with Jesus from the baptism in the Jordan onwards, and this was a condition for the choice of the replacement for Judas (*Acts 1:21-22*). When it comes to the election of assistants to the apostles in chapter 6, the apostles say it would not be right for them 'to neglect the word of God'. This may mean that they not only proclaimed, but also intensely studied the Scriptures to see how they were fulfilled in Jesus, elaborating the sort of scriptural proofs which are mentioned in the story of the road to Emmaus (*Luke 24*), and were seen in Peter's Pentecost speech.

There is no sign later in the Acts or in Paul's letters that completely common ownership existed in Christianity. In Acts 5:1-11 Ananias and Sapphira are punished not for withholding their goods but for lying that they had given them all and attempting to deceive the Spirit. As Paul made a collection for the poor of Jerusalem from the communities he had founded (Romans 15:25-26), it is clear that they had private funds.

The new Christians were also devoted to the 'fellowship' (Greek *koinonia*). We have seen how the believers addressed one another as 'brothers and sisters', forming one family. The word *koinonia* signifies community or sharing. It is elaborated in verses 44-45 that they owned everything in common and distributed among themselves according to the needs of each. Luke never ceases to point out the dangers of wealth and its misuse, and here presents an ideal of sharing rather than total communism.

Christians remained faithful to 'the breaking of bread' (Greek *he klasis tou artou*). This expression quickly became a technical term for the Eucharist, and must have this meaning here. The regular celebration of the Eucharist was a feature of the community from the beginning. The phrase in verse 46 'in their homes' is primarily contrasted with 'in the temple'. It could mean that the whole community together visited different houses, but a family celebration would be the more obvious meaning.

Finally, verse 42 speaks of fidelity to the prayers (Greek *hai proseuchai*). Attendance in the temple for the prayers mentioned in verse 46 is a sign of the continued loyalty to Judaism. There is no necessary break between Christianity and Judaism. It is noticeable that in Luke Jesus cleanses the Temple, but far more tentatively than in the other gospels (*Luke 19:45-46*). The following verse insists that he continued to preach there daily. The description of the Christians visiting the temple in Acts is enriched by the lovely word *homothumadon*, which means 'of one united heart/mind/spirit'. This is presented as characteristic of the early community.

There is no mention yet of a priest to preside, for the institution of the priesthood developed only gradually. It is surprising that the only apparent mention of an actual Eucharist in Acts is Paul's Eucharist at Troas (20:7-11). However, 1 Corinthians chapter 11 leaves no room for doubt that 'the breaking of bread' was practised from the earliest times.

The healing of the lame man

St Bede writes: The beautiful gate of the temple is the Lord. Whoever enters through him will be saved. Peter is the guide into the temple. To him, in virtue of his strong profession of faith, the epithet 'rock' and the keys of heaven were given. (Commentary on the Acts 3.2B)

v3:1 The mention of the ninth hour (3 p.m.) does not imply anything about the regular hours of prayer in the temple. We simply do not know what the custom was at that time.

v.2 We do not know which the 'Beautiful' Gate of the Temple was. Personally, I am always reminded by this story of a scene I once saw in the Ummayyad Mosque in Damascus: a crippled teenage boy lying fast asleep on a mat by the main gate, his crutches beside him, while worshippers threw coins onto his mat.

vv.3-6 Luke's message is that the Church carries on the work of Christ in the world. So it is no surprise that the apostles continue to work miracles of healing similar to those of Jesus. As Jesus cured the sick and raised the dead, so both Peter and Paul will do the same, but always in the name, that is, in the power of Jesus. In Lystra Paul cures a cripple who had never walked (*14:8-10*). Peter raises a dead woman to life in Jaffa (*9:36-42*) and Paul a dead man in Troas (*20:9-12*).

v.7 Taking the cripple by the right hand Peter 'raised him up'. Similar language, the Greek verb *egeirein*, which alludes to the resurrection, is found in many of Jesus' cures. In Mark 1:31 Jesus 'raised up' the mother-in-law of Simon Peter. The man is healed instantly.

v.8 The description of this cure is wonderfully vivid: the man 'jumped up' at Peter's grasp, 'stood' hesitantly for a moment, 'began to walk' gingerly around, and finally, as they go into the temple, he entered 'walking and leaping' in circles around them, praising God.

Opposite: St Peter and St John Healing the Paralytic, by Ramos y Albertos.

The Word Lives On

The first part of this passage (*2:36-41*) is read on Easter Tuesday, the last part (*3:1-8*) on Easter Wednesday each year. The central section about the life of the community (*2:42-47*) forms the first reading for the Second Sunday of Easter in Year A. Thus it is a passage which the Church considers important in guiding our thoughts at the beginning of Eastertide.

The early part of the passage, on the baptisms, would also make a suitable reading for a baptism of several adults.

The central part, on community life, is recommended as a reading for several occasions in religious community, such as professions and blessings of superiors. It also forms a first reading for votive Masses of the Eucharist in the Easter Season. The church therefore sees it as central in the formation of a Eucharistic community at all levels.

Peter's miraculous cure of the lame man is the first reading for the Vigil of the Solemnity of Saints Peter and Paul. It may also be used for a reading at votive Masses of the Name of Jesus in Eastertide.

The Catechism of the Catholic Church teaches:

Everything the true Christian has is to be regarded as a good possessed in common with everyone else. All Christians should be ready and eager to come to the help of the needy, and of their neighbours in want. (952)

Live the Word of God

Listen again to the reading: Acts 2:37-3:8.

Suggestions for reflection and prayer

❖ Has repentance meant anything to me in my life? Do I really have different standards from those of non-Christians around me? Have I allowed myself to be gradually corrupted?

❖ In baptism I was committed to Christ and entered into the company of Jesus. Do I truly live in the company of Jesus and do I put all my trust in him?

❖ Does my Christian society, family or parish reflect the values and *koinonia* of the first Christian community at Jerusalem? Can I do anything to improve the situation? Can I do anything to help my non-Christian surroundings benefit from these values?

❖ I can't go around dramatically healing the sick as Peter did, but do I make an effort to heal, or do I prefer to hurt? Is my first reaction to criticise and destroy, or to remedy and build up? Are people afraid of me or do they find my presence supportive?

The Venerable Bede comments on owning everything in common:

If the love of God pervades our hearts, without a doubt it will soon engender affection for our neighbour as well. Hence, because of the double ardour of one and the same love, we read that the Holy Spirit was given twice to the apostles, and the possession of everything without anyone having anything of his own is a great token of brotherly love. (Commentary on the Acts of the Apostles 2.44)

The Witness of Stephen

Hear the Word of God

Read Acts 7:44-8:1

44 Stephen said: 'Our ancestors had the tent of testimony in the wilderness, as God directed when he spoke to Moses, ordering him to make it according to the pattern he had seen. 45 Our ancestors in turn brought it in with Joshua when they dispossessed the nations that God drove out before our ancestors. And it was there until the time of David, 46 who found favour with God and asked that he might find a dwelling-place for the house of Jacob. 47 But it was Solomon who built a house for him. 48 Yet the Most High does not dwell in houses made by human hands; as the prophet says,

> 49 "Heaven is my throne,
> and the earth is my footstool.
> What kind of house will you build for me, says the Lord,
> or what is the place of my rest?
> 50 Did not my hand make all these things?"

51 'You stiff-necked people, uncircumcised in heart and ears, you are for ever opposing the Holy Spirit, just as your ancestors used to do. 52 Which of the prophets did your ancestors not persecute? They killed those who foretold the coming of the Righteous One, and now you have become his betrayers and murderers. 53 You are the ones that received the law as ordained by angels, and yet you have not kept it.'

54 When they heard these things, they became enraged and ground their teeth at Stephen. 55 But filled with the Holy Spirit, he gazed into heaven and saw the glory of God and Jesus standing at the right hand of God. 56 'Look,' he said, 'I see the heavens opened and the Son of Man standing at the right hand of God!' 57 But they covered their ears, and with a loud shout all rushed together against him. 58 Then they dragged him out of the city and began to stone him; and the witnesses laid their coats at the feet of a young man named Saul. 59 While they were stoning Stephen, he prayed, 'Lord Jesus, receive my spirit.' 60 Then he knelt down and cried out in a loud voice, 'Lord, do not hold this sin against them.' When he had said this, he died.

1 And Saul approved of their killing him. That day a severe persecution began against the church in Jerusalem, and all except the apostles were scattered throughout the countryside of Judea and Samaria.

Opposite: Killing and burial of St Stephen, by Mariotto di Nardo.

Understand the Word of God

This session will explore:

❖ the conclusion of the first era of the Church in Jerusalem

❖ Stephen's witness to the continued rebelliousness of Israel

❖ the continuing work of the Spirit

❖ Stephen's experience of the glory of God and his witness to Jesus

Setting in the Book

Since our last reading the situation of the nascent Church has progressed. Their numbers have increased, and opposition to them has developed. On two occasions apostles have been arrested and imprisoned. First, in chapter 4, Peter and John were arrested, imprisoned, brought before the Sanhedrin and given a stern warning. Then, in 5:18, 'the apostles' (all of them?) were arrested, but miraculously released, so that when the officials arrived to bring them before the Sanhedrin they were not to be found. Nevertheless, they were brought before the Sanhedrin from the temple, where they were again fearlessly proclaiming Jesus. This time they were flogged and again warned not to speak in the name of Jesus (*5:40*).

Another development has occurred. There were complaints from one group within the community, the Hellenists, or the Jews of Greek culture and language, that their widows were not receiving their fair share of the distribution of food. Seven men were appointed to serve and control the distribution. These officials seem to preach and baptise in just the same way as the apostles themselves. Were they a sort of parallel hierarchy for the Hellenists, leaving the apostles in charge of the Hebrew members of the Church? Possibly the disagreement between the Hebrews and the Hellenists was deeper than Luke is prepared to tell us.

Stephen is one of the Seven, indeed the first of the list, 'a man full of faith and the Holy Spirit' (6:5). His arrest marks the end of the Jerusalem period of the Church, for his speech of defence is one of the great speeches of Acts and sums up the efforts of the apostles to bring the Jews to faith in Christ. After the martyrdom of Stephen 'all except the apostles were scattered throughout the countryside of Judea and Samaria' (8:1). The mission to the rest of the world began, a most significant moment for the development of the Church.

What Kind of Text?

The major part of the reading is the final section of Stephen's very long speech, which goes from verse 1 to verse 53 of Acts chapter 7. As with all the set speeches in Acts, Luke, following the conventions of contemporary writers, gives us not a word-for-word transcription of what Stephen actually said, but what it would have been appropriate for him to say.

The first theme of the speech is the continuous rebelliousness of the Jews. Stephen sets out to prove his point from Scripture in a speech full of allusions and actual quotations. The second theme is the mobility of the Jewish people: they were always on the move from place to place. These themes are especially apt to the occasion, the first showing the stubbornness of Israel in rejecting Jesus, the second presaging the fact that the promise was not tied to Jerusalem and its temple, but was offered also to the Gentiles.

The final verses of our passage (7:54-8:1) narrate the martyrdom of Stephen, and display significant similarities with Luke's account of the death of Jesus.

St Augustine of Hippo writes:

Stephen was full of the Holy Spirit. He was simple, because he harmed no one; he was fervent, because he reproached the impious. When the rocks were coming down on him from their hands, on his knees he said, 'Lord, lay not this sin to their charge.' For earlier his master had done that: hanging on the cross he said, 'Father forgive them, for they know not what they do.' (Tractates on John 6.3.1-4)

The tent to which Moses went to meet the Lord, which is minutely described in Exodus 25, contained the sacred vessels, the testimony to the covenant. It represented the presence of the Lord among the people. This is why the tabernacle in which the Blessed Sacrament dwells in our churches is so called, and is often in the shape of a tent, for the Latin for 'tent' is tabernaculum.

John 4:21 'Woman, believe me, the hour is coming when you will worship the Father neither on this mountain nor in Jerusalem.'

John 4:23 'But the hour is coming, and is now here, when true worshippers will worship the Father in spirit and truth, for the Father seeks such as these to worship him.'

Commentary: verse by verse reading
The Conclusion of Stephen's Speech

v.44 Stephen has got to the stage in his speech of stressing that the 'tent of testimony', also called the 'tent of meeting', was perfectly satisfactory for the Lord. The Lord had no need of a temple, and was content to be transported around with the people in their wanderings. When David offered to build God a house, God replied that it was not for a human being to build a house for God. Rather God would build a house - a dynasty - for David. This is recounted in the Second Book of Samuel chapter 7.

vv.46-50 Stephen explains that Solomon, not David, actually built the temple. However, Stephen avoids criticising the great David, the founder of the messianic dynasty. His final point, for which he quotes the last chapter of Isaiah (*66:1-2*), is that God cannot be contained in any building. The same point will be made by Jesus when he speaks to the Samaritan woman in John chapter 4.

This life-size replica of the biblical tabernacle has been constructed in the wilderness at Timna Park, 20 miles north of Eilat in the Arabah.

vv.51-53 Stephen concludes his speech with generalisations about the history of Israel and the constant refusal of the Jews to obey the promptings of the Spirit of God in the mouths of the prophets. It is not surprising that the hearers react violently to the calculated insult that they are not really Jews at all, being 'uncircumcised in heart and ears'. The refusal to accept the prophet Jesus is only the culmination of their history, for in Luke-Acts Jesus is often presented as a prophet.

The Death of Stephen

vv.54-55 By contrast to the Jews who 'are always resisting the Holy Spirit' (verse 51), Stephen is now specially inspired by the Spirit. We have already been told that he was 'a man full of faith and the Holy Spirit' at his election (*6:3*). Barnabas and Saul are selected for their mission by the Holy Spirit, and similarly sent out by the Spirit (*13:2-4*). Paul is directed by the Spirit again and again along the course of his mission (*16:6-7*). The Spirit is always present in the Church, and we are reminded of this guidance at special grace-filled moments in the course of the story.

What is meant by Stephen seeing the glory of God? The glory of God is an awesome and daunting concept. No human being can see God and live. In his visionary experience Stephen also sees Jesus standing at the right hand of God, sharing his position and his glory, just as in the Book of Revelation the Lamb, 'standing as though slain', has his place in the midst of the divine throne (*Revelation 5:6*). It is a statement of the divinity of Christ, which will sustain Stephen in his martyrdom. It also harks back to the claim of Jesus at his trial before the Sanhedrin: 'From now on the Son of Man will be seated at the right hand of the power of God.' (*Luke 22:69*) The martyrdom of Stephen is to be the first echo in the Church of Jesus' own martyrdom.

In the synagogue at Nazareth, Jesus declares himself a prophet after the manner of Elijah and Elisha (Luke 4:16-27). 'A great prophet has risen among us', they cry after he raises the son of the widow of Nain (7:16). Jesus himself says that 'it is impossible for a prophet to be killed outside of Jerusalem' (13:33). In his ministry in Jerusalem Jesus acts as a prophet, teaching daily in the temple. Prophetic also is his triple lament over Jerusalem, as he approaches (13:34-35), as he arrives (19:41-44) and as he leaves Jerusalem (23:28-31), weeping over the coming fate of the city. Finally, his ascension is represented in terms similar to the ascension of the prophet Elijah (2 Kings 2).

When Moses asks to see the glory of God, the Lord puts him in a cleft in the rock and shields him until he has passed by, and only then calls out the name of the Lord (Exodus 33:18-34:6). At Isaiah's vision of the glory of the Lord in the temple he is bowled over by the majesty of God and shrinks away at his own unworthiness (Isaiah 6). In his opening vision, Ezekiel sees the chariot-throne and 'the appearance of the likeness of the glory of God' (Ezekiel 1:28). These are all attempts to convey the majesty and grandeur of God, which is beyond all human imagining or conception.

v.56 'I can see heaven thrown open' is also echoed by the first verse of the book of Ezekiel: 'the heavens were opened, and I saw visions of God'. In a similar way the visionary of the book of Revelation says: 'After this I looked, and there in heaven a door stood open!' (*Revelation 4:1*) Here it describes Stephen's awesome experience of the divine protection accorded to him by the Son of Man.

vv.57-58 The members of the council react to Stephen's words as to blasphemy, not least because they cannot endure the claim that heaven is supporting him. This again echoes the trial of Jesus before the Sanhedrin. Curiously, the word *homothumadon*, used in 2:46 for the unity in heart, mind and spirit of the community, reappears in verse 57 in reference to the concerted movement of his opponents against Stephen.

In John 18:31 the chief priests claim that they have no right to pass a death sentence. How then could the members of the Sanhedrin stone Stephen? The solution is either that this was a mob lynching rather than a formal execution, or that it occurred during the interregnum in 36 AD between the departure of Pilate as governor and the arrival of his successor.

Disputation of Saint Stephen, by Master of Prato.

We do not know how tight Roman control of the province of Judea was. Jerusalem was a couple of days journey away for the Roman governor, who resided at Caesarea Maritima. Nor do we know for certain how the barbaric sentence of stoning to death was carried out. Was the victim simply immobilised and pelted with stones? There is some evidence from Jewish legal traditions that the victim was hurled, bound, from a height, while the chief accuser waited below to finish the job with a boulder.

We are already shown Saul involved in the persecution of the Church, though only in an ancillary, rather than a fully murderous, capacity.

vv.59-60 Stephen's final two prayers are again reminiscent of the death of Jesus in Luke's account. They remind us that Stephen is following his Master. They echo Jesus' acceptance of the will of his Father, and the forgiveness which he offers right to the end. The first martyr for Christ witnesses not only by his proclamation of the message of the risen Christ but also by the very details of his death.

8:1 This second reference to Saul prepares for the beginning of his story in chapter 9, when he takes the road to Damascus.

Above: St Stephen's Gate in Jerusalem. This gate is so named because of the tradition that the first Christian martyr was stoned outside this gate.

St Bede comments on the martyrdom of Stephen:

The Lord, who chose us out of the world for his heavenly kingdom and glory, suffered outside the gate, like Stephen, who, as though he were a stranger to the world, was stoned outside the city. For he had no permanent city here, but with his whole heart he sought the city to come.

(Commentary on the Acts, c. 7)

Compare verses 59-60 with Luke's account of Jesus' death:

Luke 23:46 Then Jesus, crying with a loud voice, said, 'Father, into your hands I commend my spirit.'

Luke 23:34 Then Jesus said, 'Father, forgive them; for they do not know what they are doing.'

While the NRSV translation has 'Stephen died', the Greek text uses the word koimasthai which means 'to fall asleep'. St Bede comments:

It is lovely that the text says, 'He fell asleep', rather than, 'He died', for he offered a sacrifice of love and fell asleep in the hope of the resurrection. (Retractations on the Acts of the Apostles, c. 7)

The Word Lives On

The story of Stephen's martyrdom is read on Tuesday of the third week of Easter, as the story of the early Church is unfolded semi-continuously during the Easter season. It occurs also on the 7th Sunday of Easter in Year C to prepare for the gospel reading from John chapter 17 about the union of Jesus with those who will bear witness to him.

It is read also on the feast of certain martyrs, primarily St Stephen (26th December), and others such as the Martyrs of England (4th May).

Stephen's spirit of forgiveness is put before us also by its choice as a first reading in the Mass for Forgiveness of Oppressors.

The Stoning of St Stephen, by Annibale Carracci.

Live the Word of God

Listen again to the reading: Acts 7:44-8:1

Suggestions for reflection and prayer

The history of Israel, God's people, seems to be pock-marked by a series of rebellions and half-hearted returns. During all these God remains faithful.

- ❖ Is the history of the Church the same?

- ❖ Is the story of my own relationship with God the same?

Stephen's witness to the values and the dedication of Jesus was total.

- ❖ Whose witness among the lives of the saints do I find most inspiring?

- ❖ Whom do I know in the modern Church who bears similar witness, by suffering patiently borne, by patience in the face of personal difficulties with other people, by generosity to those in need, by being a refuge for others in distress, by courageously witnessing to Christ's values in the face of hostility?

- ❖ Would I have sufficient love of Christ to die for him?

Stephen ended his life forgiving those who stoned him.

- ❖ Is forgiveness always an appropriate response?

- ❖ What sort of offence do I find it hardest to forgive?

- ❖ Is there anyone I have not forgiven?

- ❖ Is there anyone of whom I should still ask forgiveness?

From a Sermon by St Fulgentius of Ruspe, which is read at the Office of Readings on the feast of St Stephen:

The love that brought Christ down from heaven to earth lifted Stephen from earth to heaven. The love that showed itself first in the king shone forth next in the soldier. And Stephen, so as to deserve to win the crown – which is what his name means – had love as his weapon and by it was utterly victorious. (Sermon 3)

The Vocation of Paul

Hear the Word of God

Read Acts 9:1-20

Meanwhile Saul, still breathing threats and murder against the disciples of the Lord, went to the high priest [2] and asked him for letters to the synagogues at Damascus, so that if he found any who belonged to the Way, men or women, he might bring them bound to Jerusalem. [3] Now as he was going along and approaching Damascus, suddenly a light from heaven flashed around him. [4] He fell to the ground and heard a voice saying to him, 'Saul, Saul, why do you persecute me?' [5] He asked, 'Who are you, Lord?' The reply came, 'I am Jesus, whom you are persecuting. [6] But get up and enter the city, and you will be told what you are to do.' [7] The men who were travelling with him stood speechless because they heard the voice but saw no one. [8] Saul got up from the ground, and though his eyes were open, he could see nothing; so they led him by the hand and brought him into Damascus. [9] For three days he was without sight, and neither ate nor drank.

[10] Now there was a disciple in Damascus named Ananias. The Lord said to him in a vision, 'Ananias.' He answered, 'Here I am, Lord.' [11] The Lord said to him, 'Get up and go to the street called Straight, and at the house of Judas look for a man of Tarsus named Saul. At this moment he is praying, [12] and he has seen in a vision a man named Ananias come in and lay his hands on him so that he might regain his sight.' [13] But Ananias answered, 'Lord, I have heard from many about this man, how much evil he has done to your saints in Jerusalem; [14] and here he has authority from the chief priests to bind all who invoke your name.' [15] But the Lord said to him, 'Go, for he is an instrument whom I have chosen to bring my name before Gentiles and kings and before the people of Israel; [16] I myself will show him how much he must suffer for the sake of my name.' [17] So Ananias went and entered the house. He laid his hands on Saul and said, 'Brother Saul, the Lord Jesus, who appeared to you on your way here, has sent me so that you may regain your sight and be filled with the Holy Spirit.' [18] And immediately something like scales fell from his eyes, and his sight was restored. Then he got up and was baptized, [19] and after taking some food, he regained his strength.

For several days he was with the disciples in Damascus, [20] and immediately he began to proclaim Jesus in the synagogues, saying, 'He is the Son of God.'

Opposite: Ananias restoring the sight of Saint Paul, by Pietro di Cortona.

Understand the Word of God

This session will explore:

❖ the nature of the story and its scriptural echoes

❖ conversion or vocation?

❖ the importance of Paul in the Christian mission

❖ Paul's suffering as Servant of the Lord Jesus

Setting in the Book

Acts 13:2 While they were worshipping the Lord and fasting, the Holy Spirit said, 'Set apart for me Barnabas and Saul for the work to which I have called them.'

The plan of the book was given in 1:8: the Good News of Jesus would be spread from Jerusalem, throughout Judaea and Samaria and indeed to earth's remotest end. The event in this reading is a crucial stage of this process, for it is Paul who will carry the message beyond the bounds of Syria-Palestine, right over the eastern Mediterranean and as far as Rome, known in Jewish literature as 'the end of the earth'. Paul would be entrusted with this mission by the Holy Spirit, speaking to the assembled community at Antioch, the great trading city in the north of Syria (*13:1-2*), where the followers of Jesus were first called 'Christians' (*11:26*).

Inside the house of St Ananias in Damascus, Syria.

So significant is the event on the road to Damascus that the story is told three times, once in chapter 9 at its occurrence, once by Paul explaining himself in the temple at Jerusalem (*chapter 22*), and once by Paul making his defence before the Roman governor, Festus, at Caesarea (*chapter 26*). This is Luke's way of drumming the lesson home, for the story of Paul's acceptance of Jesus as Messiah signals the beginning of the mission to the Gentiles. The story of the admittance of the first Gentile into the Christian community, the centurion Cornelius, will similarly be told three times to emphasise its importance (*Acts chapters 10-11 and 15*).

What Kind of Text?

Luke is a master at expressing a theological truth in historical form, or an interior event in external and dramatic form. Thus he conveys the Annunciation to Mary in a way which can be visualized and imagined – witness the many pictorial representations of what in fact was an interior revelation to Mary. In the same way he conveys this event in Paul's life in a pictorial way. This does not mean that either of these presentations is fictional. Rather he paints a scene.

We do not know what was going on in Paul's mind as he trudged towards Damascus, surely reflecting on his task and the wrongness of the followers of Jesus. There is no reason to believe that God did violence to Paul's thought-processes. It may have been a sudden flash of divine inspiration which completed his train of thought.

Luke has modelled his narrative on the story of Heliodorus in 2 Maccabees 3:25-35. Heliodorus was the hostile general of the Syrian army who came to despoil the temple. As he approached the temple he was struck down by a rearing horse ridden by a celestial young man. He was blinded and had to be carried away 'powerless to help himself'. The same young man appeared again to Heliodorus, telling him to be grateful to God for his cure. Heliodorus then offered sacrifice and testified to the works of the supreme God. The parallels with Paul's case are obvious.

Luke shows that this is the occasion of the call of Paul. It was certainly not a conversion in the sense that Paul ceased to be a Jew. He remained fiercely proud of his Jewish race and heritage to the end of his life: 'Are they Hebrews? So am I. Are they Israelites? So am I. Are they descendants of Abraham? So am I' (2 Corinthians 11:22). In his speech to the Jews in the temple (Acts 22:3) he declares his credentials: he studied under Gamaliel II, the greatest rabbinic teacher of his day, and by him was taught the exact observance of the Law. He chose the strictest way of observance. To the Sanhedrin he declares: 'Brothers, I am a Pharisee, a son of Pharisees. I am on trial concerning the hope of the resurrection of the dead.' (Acts 23:6) For Paul, Christianity is the completion, not the contradiction, of Judaism.

It may well be the same scene as is described by Paul himself in 2 Corinthians 12:2-4: 'I know a man in Christ who fourteen years ago was caught up to the third heaven – whether in the body or out of the body I do not know; God knows. And I know that such a man – whether in the body or out of the body I do not know; God knows - was caught up into Paradise and heard things that are not to be told, that no mortal is permitted to repeat.'

As in many vocation narratives of great figures in the Old Testament, there is the double call by name ('Saul, Saul', as 'Moses, Moses' in Exodus 3:4), followed by the human response ('who are you, Lord?' as 'here I am' in Exodus 3:4), followed by the divine self-identification ('I am Jesus', as 'I am the God of your ancestors' in Exodus 3:6), and the divine commission to a task.

Commentary: verse by verse reading

Paul sees the risen Jesus

vv.1-2 The dating of any event in the Acts is extremely dubious. The only firm date is provided by 18:12, when Paul was brought before the proconsul Gallio in Corinth, for we know that Gallio was proconsul of Achaia in the years 50-51 AD. This seems to have occurred not long after the Council of Jerusalem, presented in Acts 15. If this is the meeting mentioned in Galatians 2 as taking place 14 years after Paul left Jerusalem, it would mean that the event on the road to Damascus took place in the late 30s, less than ten years after the Resurrection. The description of the meeting in Galatians 2 is certainly much less formal than the Council, but they may be the same. This is the only clue we have.

The idea that the high priest could authorise Paul to arrest believers in Christ, here referred to as 'any who belonged to the Way', and bring them to Jerusalem bristles with difficulties. Did the high priest have any authority over the synagogues in Damascus, or were the letters only a request? Did the synagogue-rulers in Damascus have any power to authorise arrest of the (presumably Jewish) Christians? This seems unlikely in the highly organised Roman world.

v.3 In many popular and artistic representations of the event Paul is struck down from his horse. In none of the accounts, however, is there any mention of a horse, and such a mount would be extremely unlikely. In none of the accounts of Paul's journeyings is there mention even of a mule or a donkey. The light from heaven is an apocalyptic symbol, denoting heavenly communication.

Where we can check Luke's legal facts about Roman government of the eastern Mediterranean area, they seem to be pretty sound. For example, he gives correctly the names of the diverse magistrates in the different cities. However, in the case of Paul's proposed arrests, Luke may be filling out details inaccurately.

vv.4-6 The voice from heaven says, 'Why do you persecute me?' This expresses, and perhaps gives rise to, one of the most deep-rooted features of Paul's theology, namely the awareness that Christ is present in every Christian, that every Christian lives with Christ's own life. In the Letter to the Philippians Paul writes: 'Christ will be exalted now as always in my body, whether by life or by death. For to me, living is Christ and dying is gain.' (*1:20-21*) In Galatians 2:19-20 we read: 'I have been crucified with Christ; and it is no longer I who live, but it is Christ who lives in me.'

St Bede writes about this text:

He did not say, 'Why do you persecute my members?' but 'Why do you persecute me?' Because he is still suffering from enemies in his body, which is the church. He declared that kindnesses bestowed upon his members are also done to him when he said, 'I was hungry and you gave me to eat,' and he added in explanation, 'So long as you did it to one of the least of mine, you did it to me.' (Commentary on the Acts of the Apostles 9.4)

The Conversion of St Paul, by Michelangelo Caravaggio.

vv.7-8 The details vary in the different accounts of Paul's call. Here Paul's companions heard the voice but saw no one. In Acts 22 they saw the light, which was so dazzling that it blinded Paul but not the others, but did not hear the voice. In the briefer account in Acts 26 they all fell to the ground, and Paul heard the voice.

Such variation is not careless but in Hellenistic literature is a deliberate feature of stories re-told. Nevertheless, the image of light may well account for Paul's description of his apostolic ministry as a ministry of light. In the Second Letter to the Corinthians Paul writes: 'all of us, with unveiled faces, seeing the glory of the Lord, as though reflected in a mirror, are being transformed into the same image from one degree of glory to another' (3:18). By contrast, unbelievers cannot see 'the light of the gospel of the glory of Christ' (2 Corinthians 4:4).

St Bede comments:

Since he had not believed that the Lord had conquered death by rising on the third day, he was now taught by his own experience of the replacement of three days of darkness by the return of the light. (Commentary on the Acts of the Apostles 9.9)

It is one of the strange features of the book that no knowledge of Paul's letter-writing is even hinted at in the Acts. Did the author not know of this important aspect of Paul's apostolate? There are other surprising differences between the thought of Paul and the Acts. Paul uses the term 'apostle' for anyone who proclaims the Good News, people like Andronicus and Junia in Romans 16:7, whereas in Acts the title is only associated with those who were with Jesus from the baptism onwards (1:21-25).

More from St Bede's commentary on the story:

With the falling of the scales from his eyes under the hands of Ananias, his face showed that he had received the true light in his mind. (Commentary on the Acts of the Apostles 9.18)

v.9 The three days that Paul was without his sight may echo the three days of Jesus in the tomb before his resurrection.

Paul is baptised by Ananias

vv.10-14 One of the features of Luke's writing is 'double visions'. When the truth or the importance of a vision, or the event it portends, is to be stressed, two corresponding visions are presented. In chapter 10 Cornelius has a vision of an angel telling him to send for Peter (*Acts 10:4*), and Peter is told by the Spirit that some men have come to fetch him (*10:19*). In this passage Ananias has a vision telling him to go to Paul, and Paul has a vision of Ananias coming to lay hands on him.

v.15 Paul is to be the chosen instrument to bring the name of Jesus to both Jews and Gentiles. This is not quite what Paul says in Galatians 2:7: 'I had been entrusted with the gospel for the uncircumcised, just as Peter had been entrusted with the gospel for the circumcised'. Nevertheless, the Acts show Paul preaching to Jews and Gentiles alike, while of Peter's mission we hear no more after Acts 15. Paul proclaims the message in synagogues all over the eastern Mediterranean, and even in the temple itself.

v.16 Paul sees suffering for Christ as an integral part of his mission. It is precisely this suffering which gives him authority. He is the suffering Servant of the Lord Jesus, just as Jesus was the Suffering Servant of the Lord. He writes in the Second Letter to the Corinthians: 'Are they ministers of Christ? I am talking like a madman – I am a better one: with far greater labours, far more imprisonments, with countless floggings, and often near death.' (*2 Corinthians 11:23*)

vv.17-18 Just as in the sacraments of confirmation and ordination, the imposition of hands seems to have been already in the earliest Church a way of communicating the Spirit and appointing to an office. It is an ancient Jewish rite of conferring authority to teach and spread the message, still in use in Judaism to this day: a Rabbi is so 'ordained' by his teacher. Those appointed in chapter 6 receive the imposition of hands, either from the apostles or from the community (*6:6*). Barnabas and Saul are so confirmed in their mission by the community at Antioch (*13:3*). It is significant that this gesture was not used in the appointment of Matthias, for it was before the coming of the Spirit at Pentecost (*1:26*). He is merely 'added to the eleven apostles'.

vv. 19-20 Paul is baptised in the ordinary way and after only a few days begins to proclaim the message that 'Jesus is the Son of God'. This was always a central pillar of his message, as he writes in the great Letter to the Romans of the gospel concerning his Son, who 'was declared to be Son of God with power according to the spirit of holiness by resurrection from the dead' (*Romans 1:4*). Paul did not need to wait for full instruction in the details. He must have known beforehand the central tenets of those he was persecuting. Now he begins to proclaim what he had so vigorously denied.

A subdeacon of Rome named Arator, who died in 550 AD, produced a long Latin epic poem on the Acts of the Apostles. He writes:

God will be proclaimed to the world by this herald, and pulled from the shadows of the law, under which he was blind, he will bring light into all lands singing about the everlasting Sun. (On the Acts of the Apostles, 1)

The Chapel of St Paul is a modern stone chapel in Damascus that incorporates materials from the Bab Kisan, the ancient city gate through which Paul was lowered out of a window in Acts 9:25.

The Conversion of St Paul, by Peter Paul Rubens.

The Word Lives On

The account of the dramatic scene on the road to Damascus is of course read on the Feast of the Conversion of Paul (25th January). There is a choice between the basic account in chapter 9 and Paul's spoken defence in Jerusalem in chapter 22. Chapter 9 is also read as we work through the early history of the Church during Eastertime, on Friday of the third week of Easter. The dramatic scene features in many paintings, especially during the Renaissance and Baroque periods. The artist's imagination often runs away with him, showing Saul struck down from his horse.

Live the Word of God

Listen again to the reading: Acts 9:1-20

Suggestions for reflection and prayer

Saul's enlightenment is presented here by Luke in this dramatic form.

- ❖ What experience of the Lord's call have I had in prayer? How has this drawn me closer to him?

- ❖ What is the normal way in which we learn God's will for us? Do I listen to advice seriously given? Am I open to criticism and correction?

- ❖ Has my life really been turned round and changed by God's call?

Immediately after his baptism Paul begins to spread the Good News of Christ.

- ❖ How can I best spread the gospel message?

- ❖ Do I alienate people from Christianity by my behaviour? Is my example a help or a hindrance to others?

- ❖ How can I come nearer to being a shining example of the love of Christ for all people?

In his conversion-experience Paul was made acutely aware of the life of Christ in all his followers.

- ❖ Do I treat others as members of Christ?

- ❖ Am I aware of Christ living in me, and do I treat myself and my body with due reverence?

Collect for the Feast of the Conversion of Saint Paul:

God our Father, you taught the gospel to all the world through the preaching of Paul your apostle. May we who celebrate his conversion to the faith follow him in bearing witness to your truth. Amen

The Conversion of Cornelius

Hear the Word of God

Read Acts 10:17-36

[17] Now while Peter was greatly puzzled about what to make of the vision that he had seen, suddenly the men sent by Cornelius appeared. They were asking for Simon's house and were standing by the gate. [18] They called out to ask whether Simon, who was called Peter, was staying there. [19] While Peter was still thinking about the vision, the Spirit said to him, 'Look, three men are searching for you. [20] Now get up, go down, and go with them without hesitation; for I have sent them.' [21] So Peter went down to the men and said, 'I am the one you are looking for; what is the reason for your coming?' [22] They answered, 'Cornelius, a centurion, an upright and God-fearing man, who is well spoken of by the whole Jewish nation, was directed by a holy angel to send for you to come to his house and to hear what you have to say.' [23] So Peter invited them in and gave them lodging.

The next day he got up and went with them, and some of the believers from Joppa accompanied him. [24] The following day they came to Caesarea. Cornelius was expecting them and had called together his relatives and close friends. [25] On Peter's arrival Cornelius met him, and falling at his feet, worshipped him. [26] But Peter made him get up, saying, 'Stand up; I am only a mortal.' [27] And as he talked with him, he went in and found that many had assembled; [28] and he said to them, 'You yourselves know that it is unlawful for a Jew to associate with or to visit a Gentile; but God has shown me that I should not call anyone profane or unclean. [29] So when I was sent for, I came without objection. Now may I ask why you sent for me?'

[30] Cornelius replied, 'Four days ago at this very hour, at three o'clock, I was praying in my house when suddenly a man in dazzling clothes stood before me. [31] He said, "Cornelius, your prayer has been heard and your alms have been remembered before God. [32] Send therefore to Joppa and ask for Simon, who is called Peter; he is staying in the home of Simon, a tanner, by the sea." [33] Therefore I sent for you immediately, and you have been kind enough to come. So now all of us are here in the presence of God to listen to all that the Lord has commanded you to say.'

[34] Then Peter began to speak to them: 'I truly understand that God shows no partiality, [35] but in every nation anyone who fears him and does what is right is acceptable to him. [36] You know the message he sent to the people of Israel, preaching peace by Jesus Christ—he is Lord of all.'

Opposite: St Peter Baptising the Centurion Cornelius, by Francesco Trevisani.

Understand the Word of God

This session will explore:

- ❖ the opening of Christianity to the Gentiles
- ❖ 'God-fearers' in Judaism at the time of Jesus
- ❖ food laws and association between Jewish and Gentile Christians

Setting in the Book

Luke leaves us in no doubt that the conversion of Cornelius is one of the crucial events at the beginning of Christianity. Like the story of Paul's encounter with the risen Christ, it is repeated three times, once when it happens, once when Peter justifies his action to the apostles and believers at Jerusalem (*11:1-18*), and once, much more briefly, at the Council of Jerusalem (*15:7-9*). Why was it so important?

There were many divisions within Judaism at the time of Jesus: Pharisees, Sadducees, Essenes, Zealots and others. The followers of Jesus seemed to be just one more such group within Judaism, those who accepted Jesus as Messiah. Jesus himself does not seem to have made it clear whether all his followers needed to be Jews, or to follow a Jewish way of life.

Peter and Paul had a blazing row about whether Jewish Christians could eat with Gentile Christians (*Galatians 2:11-14*), and the new converts in Galatia were easily cowed by representatives of the Jerusalem community into returning to Jewish observances (*Galatians 1:6-7* and *3:1-3*). So it is hardly surprising that at the beginning of Acts chapter 10 Peter is thoroughly shocked by a dream-vision which tells him that it is perfectly legitimate to eat foods which he has always shunned as unclean.

As with Paul and Ananias in chapter 9, we have parallel visions. The chapter begins with the vision of Cornelius in verses 3-6 in which he is told to send for Peter, and Peter's strange vision in verses 11-16. Our text begins in verse 17, with Peter in a state of great puzzlement.

After the text examined here the story will continue with the final verses of Peter's speech, which ends in verse 43. After explaining who Jesus was he concentrates on the physical resurrection of Jesus as proof that God has appointed him the judge of everyone, alive or dead, as foretold by the prophets. It is in the name or power of Jesus that salvation is to be found.

St Peter's Church at Joppa is on the traditional site of Peter's vision.

The 'Gentile Pentecost', when the Spirit comes down on Cornelius and his household, interrupts Peter's evangelising speech (*verse 44*). The whole incident is sealed with divine approval by the spontaneous descent of the Spirit, and the same phenomena of speaking in tongues and proclaiming the glory of God as at Pentecost. This leaves no possible doubt open. They are then baptised 'in the name of Jesus Christ' (*verse 48*).

The vision of Peter in Acts 10:11-16:

Peter saw the heaven opened and something like a large sheet coming down, being lowered to the ground by its four corners. In it were all kinds of four-footed creatures and reptiles and birds of the air. Then he heard a voice saying, 'Get up, Peter; kill and eat.' But Peter said, 'By no means, Lord; for I have never eaten anything that is profane or unclean.' The voice said to him again, a second time, 'What God has made clean, you must not call profane.' This happened three times, and the thing was suddenly taken up to heaven.

Origen writes:

See how, when Peter is speaking to Cornelius, Cornelius himself and those with him were filled with the Holy Spirit. Hence, if you speak God's word and do so faithfully with a pure conscience, it can come about that while you are speaking the fire of the Holy Spirit will inflame the hearts of your hearers and immediately make them warm and eager to carry out all you are teaching. (Commentary on Romans 6.13)

What Kind of Text?

Peter's dream-vision gives heavenly authorisation to abolish the Jewish food restrictions. Peter's shock and horror at God's relaxation of his own rules - for the laws of clean and unclean food were laid down in the Torah - is wittily made plain.

Peter's reception into the house of Cornelius is equally staggering. There is the double paradox that a Roman centurion should fall at the feet of a Jewish fisherman, and that an observant Jew should enter a Gentile house.

The fact that the first Gentile to be received into the Church is a Roman officer is surely significant. By the time Luke was writing there had already occurred spasmodic persecution of Christians by the Romans. Luke is therefore concerned to show again and again that harmonious relationships could and did exist between Christians and Rome. Neither had anything to fear from the other.

In the Roman Empire Judaism was a religio licita*, that is, it was exempt from the prohibitions on associations and gatherings which might be considered threatening to the Empire. As Christianity progressively split off from Judaism towards the end of the first century, it no longer enjoyed the protection of this freedom.*

Luke reports that Roman officials are often favourably impressed by Paul. The proconsul of Cyprus becomes a believer in 13:32. Paul is protected by the proconsul of Achaia in 18:15, and the Roman tribune in the temple in chapters 21-22. Finally, Paul even appeals to Caesar against the murderous threats of his own fellow-countrymen.

Sarcophagus of Marcia Romania Celsa: Baptism of Cornelius, Arles.

Commentary: verse by verse reading
The visions of Peter and Cornelius

vv.17-23 Peter's pre-prandial midday siesta produced a hunger-dream of extreme significance. The laws about clean and unclean food were notionally laid down before the Flood, and we read in Genesis 7:2 of the distinction between clean and unclean. These laws have served as a distinctive boundary-marker for observant Jews from the Babylonian Exile onwards. Many of them are based on hygiene and the avoidance of contamination (*Leviticus 11*), and others are intended to outlaw magical Canaanite practices, such as boiling a kid in its mother's milk (*Exodus 23:19*).

Cornelius was first introduced in 10:1: 'In Caesarea there was a man named Cornelius, a centurion of the Italian Cohort, as it was called.' Verse 2 continued: 'He was a devout man who feared God with all his household; he gave alms generously to the people and prayed constantly to God.'

The *Italica* cohort in which Cornelius was an officer would have been a detachment of auxiliary troops, presumably from Italy. There were no legions stationed in Palestine until after the Jewish revolt in 70 AD. Cornelius is described as 'God-fearing' (*verse 22*). Such individuals were loosely attached to Judaism, presumably attracted by its firm monotheism, by contrast to the depravities of Greco-Roman religion, and by the prayer and strict moral code of Judaism. They did not undergo circumcision. There were many 'God-fearers' in the Roman world, and it was from these that numbers of converts were attracted to Christianity.

From St Bede's commentary:
At the sixth hour, in the midst of his prayer, Peter became hungry – hungry indeed for the salvation of the world - which in the sixth age the Lord had come to seek and to save. Christ himself also wished to indicate this when, at the same hour of the day, he became thirsty at the Samaritan well. (Commentary on the Acts of the Apostles 10.9)

Speaking in Antioch in Pisidia Paul addresses those assembled in the synagogue as follows: 'You Israelites, and others who fear God, listen.' (Acts 13:16)

Peter goes to Caesarea

v.24 Caesarea Maritima was the capital of the Roman province of Judaea, the seat of the governor and the administrative centre. The port and town formed one of the most magnificent building projects of Herod the Great. He constructed a sheltered harbour by making a harbour bar. His great warehouses, theatre and aqueduct bringing fresh water into the city are visible to this day. The whole was inaugurated by a great festival of games in honour of Caesar in 10 BC.

Not only are Peter and Paul the two obvious leaders in the two halves of the book of Acts, but they each cure a lame man (3:1 and 13:8), each triumph over a magician (8:9 and 13:6), each raise the dead (9:36 and 20:9), and each is miraculously set free from prison (12:6 and 16:24).

vv.25-27 The word used for 'worshipped him' in verse 25 properly denotes reverence done to God. It is a striking part of the parallel in Acts between Peter and Paul that each receives and refuses divine honours. In Paul's case this happens when he and Barnabas are mistaken for Hermes and Zeus at Iconium *(Acts 14:11-15)*.

Caesarea Maritima - This site was insignificant until Herod the Great began to develop it into a magnificent harbour befitting his kingdom. The harbour was built using materials that would allow the concrete to harden under water. The forty-acre harbour would accommodate 300 ships, much larger than the modern harbour existing today.

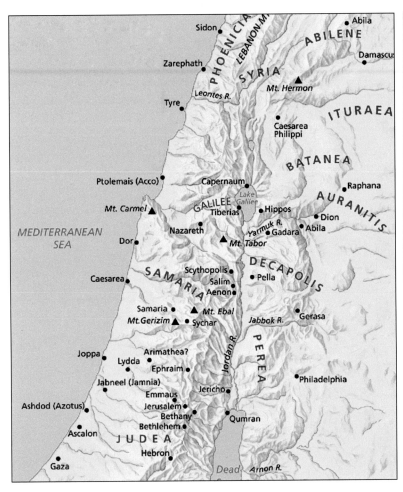

Map showing Caesarea.

vv.28-29 Peter's opening conversation concentrates on the unmistakable indications of two points, that Gentiles also are acceptable to God, and that it is perfectly legitimate for Jews and Gentiles to mingle together. To prove the point, he even lodges for some days with Cornelius (*verse 48*).

vv.30-33 We know little about Jewish hours of prayer at this time. Daniel, who is a model of strict observance, prayed three times a day (*Daniel 6:11*), and Cornelius may have been following a Jewish custom when he prayed at three o'clock which is literally 'the ninth hour'.

vv.34-36 Peter goes on to affirm that 'God shows no partiality, but in every nation anyone who fears him and does what is right is acceptable to him'. This is the charter for the opening of Christianity to the Gentiles.

St Bede writes:

It is fitting that it was at the ninth hour that Cornelius received the divine message concerning the baptism he was to ask for, since he was to be baptised in the death of the one who sent forth his spirit at the ninth hour. (Commentary on the Acts of the Apostles 10.3)

The Word Lives On

Excerpts from the story of the conversion of Cornelius are read on the Sixth Sunday of Easter in Year B, as part of the preparation for the coming of the Spirit at Pentecost. It is also one of the readings suggested for the sacrament of Confirmation.

On the Feast of the Baptism of the Lord, the reading of Acts 10:34-38 is chosen due to its reference to the baptism of Jesus, his 'anointing with the Holy Spirit'.

At Prayer During the Day in the Liturgy of the Hours the concluding prayer at midday on Tuesdays in ordinary time states: 'Almighty God, you revealed to Peter your plan for the salvation of all'. This is a clear allusion to the noon vision of Peter in the early verses of Acts 10. The concluding prayer for Prayer During the Day when recited on Tuesdays in the afternoon alludes to the angel sent to Cornelius 'at the ninth hour'. It reads: 'Almighty God, we recall how you sent your angel to the centurion Cornelius to show him the way of salvation.'

In similar fashion, the visit to the temple of Peter and John for the hour of prayer 'at the ninth hour', recounted in Acts 3:1, is recalled at Prayer During the Day on Mondays in ordinary time. The ancient tradition of Christian prayer throughout the day delights in making these connections.

The Catechism of the Catholic Church states:

The gathering together of the Church is, as it were, God's reaction to the chaos provoked by sin. This reunification is achieved secretly in the heart of all peoples: 'In every nation anyone who fears him and does what is right is acceptable' to God. (761)

Live the Word of God

Listen again to the reading: Acts 10:17-36

Suggestions for reflection and prayer

In the course of Christian history relationships between Gentiles and Jews have often been difficult. Anti-Semitism has been a recurrent feature in Christian countries, culminating in tolerance by some Christians of Hitler's persecution of the Jews.

- ❖ What is the status of Jews in God's eyes? Are Jews still in any way 'the chosen people' or have they lost this privilege by failure to accept the Messiah?
- ❖ Do I treat Jewish believers as brothers (or at least cousins) in the faith of Abraham?
- ❖ The Vatican Council text given in the margin insists that believers of other traditions, both within and beyond Christianity, belong in various ways to Christ's Church. Do I give other faiths the respect which is their due?

The Church recognises that it is linked to others who are baptized Christians, though not sharing the full faith of the Church nor unity with the successor of Peter. Those who have not yet received the gospel are also related to the People of God. Firstly, the people from whom Christ was born remain most dear to God. Others, too, acknowledge the Creator. Nor is God far distant from those who in shadows and images seek the unknown God. (Dogmatic Constitution on the Church of the Second Vatican Council, Lumen Gentium, 15-16)

The Jewish food-laws and other regulations served to express and foster devotion to the Lord, in much the same way as many Christian devotional practices.

- ❖ Do I give due value to such Christian and Catholic practices?
- ❖ Have such practices become purely automatic in my life, or even disappeared: holy water, genuflection, prayer at mealtimes, fasting before Communion?

Relationships between Christianity and the Roman Empire were not always as peaceful as Luke represents them.

- ❖ In the modern world what should the relationship between Church and State be? Is a Church established by law desirable? What should a Christian's attitude to a persecuting state be?
- ❖ How much responsibility should a Christian take for the expression of Christian values in government and administration? How important is it to take a stand, even a public stand, on such matters as abortion laws, civil partnerships, assisted suicide? Is this a duty or an option?
- ❖ How important is it to take an interest and play a part in civic affairs?

The Council of Jerusalem

Hear the Word of God

Read Acts 15:1-12 and 22-29

Then certain individuals came down from Judea and were teaching the brothers, 'Unless you are circumcised according to the custom of Moses, you cannot be saved.' [2] And after Paul and Barnabas had no small dissension and debate with them, Paul and Barnabas and some of the others were appointed to go up to Jerusalem to discuss this question with the apostles and the elders. [3] So they were sent on their way by the church, and as they passed through both Phoenicia and Samaria, they reported the conversion of the Gentiles, and brought great joy to all the believers. [4] When they came to Jerusalem, they were welcomed by the church and the apostles and the elders, and they reported all that God had done with them. [5] But some believers who belonged to the sect of the Pharisees stood up and said, 'It is necessary for them to be circumcised and ordered to keep the law of Moses.'

[6] The apostles and the elders met together to consider this matter. [7] After there had been much debate, Peter stood up and said to them, 'My brothers, you know that in the early days God made a choice among you, that I should be the one through whom the Gentiles would hear the message of the good news and become believers. [8] And God, who knows the human heart, testified to them by giving them the Holy Spirit, just as he did to us; [9] and in cleansing their hearts by faith he has made no distinction between them and us. [10] Now therefore why are you putting God to the test by placing on the neck of the disciples a yoke that neither our ancestors nor we have been able to bear? [11] On the contrary, we believe that we will be saved through the grace of the Lord Jesus, just as they will.'

[12] The whole assembly kept silence, and listened to Barnabas and Paul as they told of all the signs and wonders that God had done through them among the Gentiles.

[22] Then the apostles and the elders, with the consent of the whole church, decided to choose men from among their members and to send them to Antioch with Paul and Barnabas. They sent Judas called Barsabbas, and Silas, leaders among the brothers, [23] with the following letter: 'The brothers, both the apostles and the elders, to the believers of Gentile origin in Antioch and Syria and Cilicia, greetings. [24] Since we have heard that certain persons who have gone out from us, though with no instructions from us, have said things to disturb you and have unsettled your minds, [25] we have decided unanimously to choose representatives and send them to you, along with our beloved Barnabas and Paul, [26] who have risked their lives for the sake of our Lord Jesus Christ. [27] We have therefore sent Judas and Silas, who themselves will tell you the same things by word of mouth. [28] For it has seemed good to the Holy Spirit and to us to impose on you no further burden than these essentials: [29] that you abstain from what has been sacrificed to idols and from blood and from what is strangled and from fornication. If you keep yourselves from these, you will do well. Farewell.'

Opposite: Predella panel with Saint Peter Apostle Preaching, by Lorenzo Veneziano.

Understand the Word of God

This session will explore:

❖ the historical difficulty of a Church of Jews and Gentiles

❖ the importance of this meeting of what was then the universal Church

❖ Luke's care to underline the harmony prevalent in the Church

Setting in the Book

The Council of Jerusalem is another important growth-point in the history of the early Church. The very fact of the return to Jerusalem alerts the reader to that, for in Luke's mind Jerusalem is always a city of high significance. It is the first time for some chapters that we have had a full view of the activities of the Church in this original and ideal community. It is also the last time Peter, in some ways the hero of the first part of Acts, appears in the story.

Perhaps most important of all, the crucial phrase also occurs, 'It has seemed good to the Holy Spirit and to us', which will for ever mark the consciousness and confidence of the Church in being guided in its task of leadership and teaching by the Holy Spirit.

Not only does the rightly so-called 'Council of Jerusalem' serve as a fine example of a Church discussion, but it is also a central point of the theology and development of the Church. It is placed centrally in the book, after the preliminaries of the vocation of the Apostle of the Gentiles in chapter 9 and Peter's action in receiving the Gentile Cornelius in chapter 10. It clears the way for Paul to proceed on his world-mission, the mission which occupies the remainder of the book and completes the plan given in Acts 1:8.

Luke presents a sort of paradigm of a community decision on an important matter. Disagreement is referred to the mother-Church at Jerusalem, the centre of unity, delegates being sent to represent the different points of view. The community meets to discuss the matter.

Advice is given by the leaders of the community, not entirely in agreement. A discussion follows, concluding with a decision by the whole community, in explicit awareness of the presence and participation of the Holy Spirit. Finally, the decision is communicated and received with joy.

What Kind of Text?

By now we are accustomed to the fact that Luke composes in many different ways, and that he is a master of creating a scene from disparate materials. Is this account of the 'Council' an account of one event or does it combine a series of decisions at different times? How does it relate to the visit to Jerusalem of Paul and Barnabas reported in Galatians 2:1-2, which is described by Paul as 'a private meeting with the acknowledged leaders'? Is the letter with which the account in Acts concludes derived from a different occasion and tacked on here somewhat awkwardly? Is it a majestic formalisation of a series of discussions and disputes?

An initial historical difficulty is that the issue which led to the community at Antioch sending Paul and Barnabas up to the mother-church at Jerusalem was whether Christians needed to become full Jews, whether they needed to be circumcised. As we have seen, a number of the new converts were from the ranks of the 'God-fearers', who would not have already embraced circumcision, and would no doubt not be eager to undergo this painful operation. However, once the meeting happens, no discussion or decision occurs about circumcision.

Paul writes in Galatians 2:1-2: Then after fourteen years I went up again to Jerusalem with Barnabas, taking Titus along with me. I went up in response to a revelation. Then I laid before them (though only in a private meeting with the acknowledged leaders) the gospel that I proclaim among the Gentiles, in order to make sure that I was not running, or had not run, in vain.

The Second Vatican Council met in Rome from 1962 to 1965.

In his encyclical letter Redemptoris Missio *on the missionary activity of the Church, promulgated in 1990, Blessed John Paul II wrote: The Holy Spirit is indeed the principal agent of the whole of the Church's mission. His action is preeminent in the mission* ad gentes, *as can clearly be seen in the early Church: in the conversion of Cornelius (Acts 10), in the decisions made about emerging problems (Acts 15) and in the choice of regions and peoples to be evangelised (Acts 16:6ff). (21)*

Peter's speech in verses 7-11 concerns the related but broader issue, whether Gentiles should be received at all. His decision, based on the descent of the Holy Spirit on Cornelius because of his faith, is that the Law is simply an unnecessary and insupportable burden.

After the speech of Peter the assembly listens to Barnabas and Paul and their testimony of the Gentile mission. James' words, found in verses 13-21, are not included in our chosen text. The four matters he mentions in verse 20 seem to be conditions of association between Jews and Gentiles.

While Paul and Barnabas are sent up to Jerusalem for a decision specifically about circumcision of Gentile converts to Christianity, Luke makes this the occasion for a third mention of the welcome given by the Holy Spirit to Gentile believers, a much more fundamental matter. The solution is that faith in the Risen Christ makes Jewish observance superfluous. In Christ's resurrection the promises to Abraham are so fulfilled that Jewish observance can be discarded, like the launch capsule of a space-rocket.

James became the leader of the Jerusalem church.

Commentary: verse by verse reading

Paul and Barnabas go up to Jerusalem

vv.1-5 The action in this chapter begins in Antioch, now just on the Syrian side of the border with Turkey, which was possibly the most important trading-port of the eastern Mediterranean littoral, the end of the land trading-route from China, India and the East. There had been an important Jewish colony there since the third century BC, and they enjoyed special privileges granted by the Emperor. They lived in a quarter of the city called Daphne, described by one archaeologist as 'the Beverley Hills of Antioch'.

In Antioch the followers of Jesus were first called 'Christians' (*11:26*). From there was made the startling innovation, not at all customary within Judaism, of sending out missionaries, Barnabas and Saul, to spread the Good News of Jesus (*13:2-3*). Clearly the Church at Jerusalem felt that they had some sort of oversight of this innovative young community.

The question arises whether the 'certain individuals' sent from Judea in verse 1 are the same as those mentioned in Galatians 2:12, people who came to insist that Jew and Gentile should not eat together. This led to Peter abandoning his habit of eating with Gentiles. It is possible that people from the Jerusalem church may have intervened on more than one occasion.

It is notable that Barnabas was originally the leader of the two (Barnabas and Saul in *Acts 13:2*), but by Acts 15 the position has been reversed. Acts 15:39 makes clear that after a row at Antioch they split up. They may have been chosen as delegates to represent two opposing viewpoints.

Despite these differences of view, Luke is always eager to underline the harmony and mutual support within the churches. There is an atmosphere of joy and thanksgiving for the spread of the gospel in verses 3-4.

Acts 13:2-3: While they were worshipping the Lord and fasting, the Holy Spirit said, 'Set apart for me Barnabas and Saul for the work to which I have called them.' Then after fasting and praying they laid their hands on them and sent them off.

Galatians 2:11-13: But when Cephas (Peter) came to Antioch, I opposed him to his face, because he stood self-condemned; for until certain people came from James, he used to eat with the Gentiles. But after they came, he drew back and kept himself separate for fear of the circumcision faction. And the other Jews joined him in this hypocrisy, so that even Barnabas was led astray by their hypocrisy.

Debate and decision

vv.6-12 Once the apostles and elders have gathered, it is Peter who speaks first. There is a dangerous little divergence here: Peter thinks the mission to the Gentiles was entrusted to him. Paul has a different idea, and in Galatians 2:8 he writes: 'he who worked through Peter making him an apostle to the circumcised also worked through me in sending me to the Gentiles'!

The allusion to the Cornelius incident is not so much an account as a theological analysis: Jews no longer have a privileged position. Only faith is required for salvation. Here faith is, of course, a matter not of detailed belief, but of putting one's whole trust in the Lord Jesus. Nor is 'grace' a matter of spiritual fuel. It is a free gift lavished by the Lord, an expression of a personal relationship.

vv.22-29 For reasons of space we have been obliged to omit the speech of James, in which he expresses his agreement with 'Simeon' (the Hebrew version of Simon Peter's name).

The letter, in verses 23-29, is gently and tactfully written, deploring any upset which might have occurred, stressing the unanimity of the decision, praising the original delegates, underlining the care not to impose any unnecessary burden, and finally assuming the goodwill of the recipients.

If it is correct that Paul and Barnabas were chosen to represent the two points of view, Paul that of freedom for the Gentiles, Barnabas that of retention of the Jewish Law, it is interesting to note the continuance of this evenly-balanced stance in the delegates chosen to accompany the letter, listed in verse 22. Judas Barsabbas, whose very name is so Jewish, no doubt represents the Jewish point of view, while Silas/Silvanus is several times mentioned as a companion of Paul on his missionary journeys. Starting from their different viewpoints, they must, however, have reached agreement in supporting the decision.

St Bede writes: There is no need of circumcision of the flesh to cleanse those whose hearts were purified by so much faith that, even before baptism, they deserved to receive the Holy Spirit. (Commentary on the Acts of the Apostles 15.9)

The first part of the speech, agreeing with Peter, must have been composed by Luke and attributed to James by him, since it uses the Greek version of the Bible rather than the Hebrew. The second part of James' speech suggests the restrictions expressed in the letter. They are listed in the order in which they occur in Leviticus 17:18, as the rules for Gentiles living among Jews, for them to avoid upsetting the Jews.

St Cyril of Jerusalem teaches: They indicated clearly by what they wrote that though the decree had been written by men who were apostles, it was from the Holy Spirit and universal. Barnabas and Paul took this decree and confirmed it to the whole world. (Catechetical Lecture 17.29)

Opposite: Scenes from the Life of Saint Barnabas and his Martyrdom, by Florentine School.

The Word Lives On

Excerpts from the account of the Council of Jerusalem are read on the Sixth Sunday of Easter in Year C, as preparation for the coming of the Spirit at Pentecost. A fuller, almost continuous, reading occurs as part of the Easter-time history of earliest Christianity in the weekdays of the fifth week of Easter (Wednesday to Friday) each year.

In his encyclical letter on ecumenism, issued in 1995, Blessed John Paul II wrote: This journey towards the necessary and sufficient visible unity, in the communion of the one Church willed by Christ, continues to require patient and courageous efforts. In this process, one must not impose any burden beyond that which is strictly necessary (Acts 15:28). (Ut Unum Sint 78)

In the Decree on Ecumenism of the Second Vatican Council (*Unitatis Redintegratio*) the Council adopts the same pastoral approach which is found in Acts 15 in developing relations with the Eastern Churches. We read: 'After taking all these factors into consideration, this Sacred Council solemnly repeats the declaration of previous Councils and Roman Pontiffs, that for the restoration or the maintenance of unity and communion it is necessary "to impose no burden beyond what is essential" (*Acts 15:28*). It is the Council's urgent desire that, in the various organizations and living activities of the Church, every effort should be made toward the gradual realization of this unity, especially by prayer, and by fraternal dialogue on points of doctrine and the more pressing pastoral problems of our time.'

Pope Paul VI meets Patriarch Athenagoras in 1964 in Jerusalem.

Live the Word of God

Listen again to the reading: Acts 15:1-12 and 22-29

Suggestions for reflection and prayer

The consciousness of the guidance of the Holy Spirit broods over the account of this first Council or Synod of the Church.

❖ The Holy Spirit is still present in the deliberations of the Church, and especially in the general Councils of the Church, such as Vatican II. But the Spirit is also present when Christians meet together – 'there am I in the midst of them' (Matthew 18:20).

❖ The Spirit is present in the guidance of the bishops, priests and all other ministers of the Church. I need to remember this in my reception of such guidance, and also in the way I act as a minister of the Church – whatever my ministry may be.

❖ How does the voice of the Spirit normally come to me? Through my pastors and teachers, through my friends, and especially my critics, through my family (especially when I have annoyed them)?

The story of the Council of Jerusalem begins in disagreement and ends in harmonious agreement.

❖ How can the Church continue to repeat this transformation?

❖ Do I set about securing peace and harmony in my Christian (and other) activities, or do I domineer and push through my own opinion in the face of opposition?

❖ Do I set about discussions with due reflection and prayer on the will of God and the guidance of the Spirit?

We read about the action of the Holy Spirit:

The Spirit prepares men and women and goes out to them with his grace, in order to draw them to Christ. The Spirit manifests the risen Lord to them, recalls his word to them and opens their minds to the understanding of his death and Resurrection. He makes present the mystery of Christ, supremely in the Eucharist, in order to reconcile them, to bring them into communion with God, that they may bear much fruit. (Catechism of the Catholic Church, 737)

Paul's Speech to the Athenians

Hear the Word of God

Read Acts 17:16-34

16 While Paul was waiting for them in Athens, he was deeply distressed to see that the city was full of idols. 17 So he argued in the synagogue with the Jews and the devout persons, and also in the market-place every day with those who happened to be there. 18 Also some Epicurean and Stoic philosophers debated with him. Some said, 'What does this babbler want to say?' Others said, 'He seems to be a proclaimer of foreign divinities.' (This was because he was telling the good news about Jesus and the resurrection.) 19 So they took him and brought him to the Areopagus and asked him, 'May we know what this new teaching is that you are presenting? 20 It sounds rather strange to us, so we would like to know what it means.' 21 Now all the Athenians and the foreigners living there would spend their time in nothing but telling or hearing something new.

22 Then Paul stood in front of the Areopagus and said, 'Athenians, I see how extremely religious you are in every way. 23 For as I went through the city and looked carefully at the objects of your worship, I found among them an altar with the inscription, "To an unknown god." What therefore you worship as unknown, this I proclaim to you. 24 The God who made the world and everything in it, he who is Lord of heaven and earth, does not live in shrines made by human hands, 25 nor is he served by human hands, as though he needed anything, since he himself gives to all mortals life and breath and all things. 26 From one ancestor he made all nations to inhabit the whole earth, and he allotted the times of their existence and the boundaries of the places where they would live, 27 so that they would search for God and perhaps grope for him and find him—though indeed he is not far from each one of us. 28 For "In him we live and move and have our being"; as even some of your own poets have said, "For we too are his offspring."

29 Since we are God's offspring, we ought not to think that the deity is like gold, or silver, or stone, an image formed by the art and imagination of mortals. 30 While God has overlooked the times of human ignorance, now he commands all people everywhere to repent, 31 because he has fixed a day on which he will have the world judged in righteousness by a man whom he has appointed, and of this he has given assurance to all by raising him from the dead.'

32 When they heard of the resurrection of the dead, some scoffed; but others said, 'We will hear you again about this.' 33 At that point Paul left them. 34 But some of them joined him and became believers, including Dionysius the Areopagite and a woman named Damaris, and others with them.

Opposite: St Paul Preaching at Athens, by Raphael.

Understand the Word of God

This session will explore:

❖ the noble but jaded city of Athens in Paul's day

❖ Luke's brilliant literary skill as shown in this speech

❖ the possibility of discovering God through nature

❖ the importance of women in early Christianity

Setting in the Book

Acts 16:9-10 recounts Paul's vision of a Macedonian asking for help: During the night Paul had a vision. There stood a man of Macedonia pleading with him and saying, 'Come over to Macedonia and help us.' When he had seen the vision, we immediately tried to cross over to Macedonia, being convinced that God had called us to proclaim the good news to them.

Since the Council of Jerusalem, Paul has made massive progress. He has split up from Barnabas, possibly over disagreement about Jewish observance, but Luke is not eager to tell us about disagreements within the Church. Paul has formed his own team, who all, like Silas and Timothy, have Greek names. Guided at every step by the Holy Spirit, he has journeyed overland through Asia Minor, and then made the significant move of crossing into Greece. In each place he has proclaimed the Good News first in the synagogue, made a few converts, but repeatedly been rejected by the majority of Jews.

Eventually he comes to Athens, and there Luke gives us what is possibly the most carefully-honed speech in the whole book. It is intended as a prime example of Paul's proclamation to the Gentiles, wholly different from his preaching to the Jews, before whom he could rely on considerable biblical background.

But it is more than this, for Athens still had the reputation of being the intellectual capital of the Roman Empire. It had in its own day been an imperial capital, and presumably still had the lingering aura of a decayed world-capital, like Alexandria, Naples, Rome, Constantinople, possibly London. It was still an intellectual capital, a university centre at which the sons of prominent Romans would be educated, for the Greeks had the reputation in the Roman Empire of being the philosophers and educators, excelling in wit and polish as well as cunning, and providing most of the tutors, doctors and thinkers in the Roman world. Paul would therefore be on his mettle – and so is Luke!

What Kind of Text?

On the one hand, this speech is composed in the convention of Hellenistic historians. That is to say, it does not even purport to be a first-hand report of what was actually said by Paul, for convention dictated that such speeches were not so much what *was* said as what *should have been* said, what was appropriate to the occasion. On the other hand, one of the skills taught in every school of rhetoric was *prosopopoiea*, the art of accommodating an artificial speech to the speaker.

Paul's speech before the Athenians is a masterpiece, combining three objectives. First, it is an example of a *kerygmatic* speech to the Gentiles, a proclamation of the Good News of Christ to those who lacked any biblical background. Secondly, it is in the Pauline mould of thought, so that many of the lines taken are found also in Paul's own letters, notably the first chapter of the Letter to the Romans. Thirdly, it is a masterpiece of irony. On the surface it is full of flattery for the intellectual giants of the age in the Council of the Areopagus, the assembly of the leading citizens of Athens, the leading intellectual city of the world. Beneath the surface, however, it subtly makes fun of them and their pretensions.

A brilliant example of an artificial speech is one attributed to the Emperor Claudius by Tacitus, for Claudius had the reputation of being a prosy old antiquarian, who could bore his audiences out of their minds! This is admirably caught by the historian Tacitus! Luke has this art to perfection, so Paul's speech to the Jews at Antioch, in 13:17-41, is a brilliant example of a rabbinic homily in the first-century style, technically known as a yelammadenu *homily.*

The Greek words Areios Pagos *referred to the hill to the west of the Acropolis in Athens. This was the 'hill of Ares', the Greek god of war. It was used for public speeches. It also gave its name to the supreme judicial council of the city. A bronze plaque on the hill today gives the Greek text of Paul's speech.*

The Areopagus (Mars' Hill).

Commentary: verse by verse reading

Paul in Athens

v.16 The opening clue is given in Paul's disgust at the idolatry he finds in Athens. Athens was, of course, the centre of traditional Greek religion, which, by contrast to Jewish and Christian monotheism, had a god for every aspect of life: Cybele for agriculture, Hephaistos for metal-working, Aphrodite for love, Hebe for child-birth, Ares for war. The legends of these gods were full of every sort of sexual and other misbehaviour, so that by now they had been thoroughly discredited, though they still held a place in civic celebrations.

vv.17-18 The supercilious complacency of the Epicurean and Stoic philosophers is palpable. They think Paul a fool, but he will soon show his superiority to them. Their contemptuous remark could be translated, 'What on earth could this seed-picker (Greek *spermologos*) be trying to say?' They mock Paul as a scavenger-bird which picks up seeds wherever it can. It falls back on themselves, for all Christians know the significance of the parable of the seed.

Their next smart remark also falls back on themselves: they mock Paul for introducing new male and female deities, Jesus and Anastasis ('Resurrection', feminine in form). But they seem to have forgotten that their own favourite philosopher, Socrates, was unjustly condemned for introducing new-fangled gods. Luke is mocking the contemptuous Athenians at every turn.

vv.19-21 So we come to the climax, the speech on the renowned and awesome hill of the Areopagus. Their one amusement is to discuss and listen to the latest ideas. Yes, and how bad their assessment of them is going to turn out to be!

St Bede comments on the different groups as follows:

The Epicureans, following the stupidity of their teacher, put the happiness of humanity in the pleasure of the body alone, while the Stoics placed it solely in the virtue of the mind. Although indeed they disagreed with each other, they nevertheless were united in opposition to the apostle with respect to his belief that a human being subsists in soul and body. Thus Paul taught that one ought to be happy in both body and soul, but that this will not be achieved in the present time or by human power, but by the grace of God through Jesus Christ, in the glory of the resurrection. (Commentary on the Acts, c. 17)

Paul's speech

vv.22-23 Paul begins his speech with a standard rhetorical ploy of a *captatio benevolentiae*, flattering his audience to win their goodwill, using his tourist's observations of monuments to compliment them on their religious sense, or so it seems. In fact the word translated complimentarily 'religious' can also mean 'superstitious' (Greek *deisidaimonesteroi*, literally 'scared of demons'). The Athenians would be flattered by the former meaning, but of course Paul means the latter.

They put up altars 'To Unknown Gods' out of superstitious fear that among all the gods they might have missed some out. By putting it in the singular, 'To an Unknown God', Paul is hinting at their pitiable ignorance of the one God who does exist. They have in fact missed out the one true God.

vv.24-25 Paul now reverts to the standard biblical polemic against gods 'made by human hands', especially familiar from the Babylonian exile onwards. This passage bears a striking similarity to the argument against idols in Romans 1:20-23. Again, Paul's argument that God is not in need of anything and cannot be served by human hands should have been thoroughly familiar to the Athenian philosophers, for it is Socrates' basic premise in Plato's dialogue *Euthyphro*.

vv.26-27 Paul takes issue with, or rather trumps, the Epicureans. They held that everything comes from one 'principle', and so stressed the unity of all peoples. Paul's expression could mean this, but also that the whole human race came from one 'ancestor', namely Adam. He shows therefore that the Epicurean idea is in perfect harmony with the biblical teaching, also a Pauline teaching which is vital for the argument in Romans 5 on the First and Second Adam.

The natural theology of these verses is the positive heart of the speech, insisting that some concept of God may be derived from serious contemplation of the universe. It is also a very Pauline idea, the foundation of his strictures in Romans 1:20 against those Gentiles for whom 'the eternal power and divine nature of God, invisible though

Romans 1:20-23

Ever since the creation of the world God's eternal power and divine nature, invisible though they are, have been understood and seen through the things he has made. So they are without excuse; for though they knew God, they did not honour him as God or give thanks to him, but they became futile in their thinking, and their senseless minds were darkened. Claiming to be wise, they became fools; and they exchanged the glory of the immortal God for images resembling a mortal human being or birds or four-footed animals or reptiles.

they are' should have been 'understood and seen through the things God has made'.

The phrase 'he allotted the times of their existence and the boundaries of the places where they would live' in verse 26 may suggest that the author favours the classic argument from Order as a means of discovering the deity. On the other hand, 'he is not far from each one of us' might even suggest Newman's argument from Conscience.

It would, however, be a mistake to tie the author down too tightly to particular arguments of natural theology, especially in view of the delicately phrased, 'and perhaps grope for him and find him'. The image is of blind people successfully feeling their way. The discovery of God in nature is indeed possible and valuable, but the image of the blind feeling their way towards God is very apt.

vv.28-29 Paul turns to the Stoics, alluding to Epimenides of Cnossos by his 'in him we live and move and have our being', and quoting the third-century BC Stoic poet Aratus, 'We are his offspring'. Paul's reasoning ends with the warning that we should be able to see that God is not like anything human or created. If we bring God down to the level of anything created, we grievously distort our conception of the divine.

St John Chrysostom comments: What Paul means is this. Not only did he give 'life and breath and everything', but also the sum and total of everything: he led people to the knowledge of himself, giving us the means through which we can find him and understand him. (Homilies on the Acts of the Apostles 38)

Bede writes: We are very rightly called the offspring of God, not in the sense that we were brought forth out of his nature but in the sense that through his Spirit we are both created by his will and recreated by his adoption. (Commentary on the Acts of the Apostles 17:28)

School of Athens, from the Stanza della Segnatura, by Raphael.

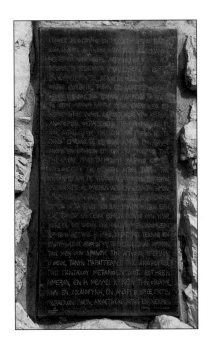

vv.30-31 Paul concludes his speech with an appeal to repentance, just as Peter concluded his early kerygmatic speeches. A particularly Pauline touch is the mention of God overlooking times of ignorance, strikingly similar to the statement in Romans 3:25, that in times past sins had gone unpunished because God held his hand.

Paul's last words refer to the resurrection of Christ from the dead and his coming as judge. Altogether, the speech is a masterpiece of rhetorical mockery and irony, as well as a firm appeal to the Athenian philosophers, based on their own revered masters.

Paul also makes a final neat little rhetorical flourish with the repeated 'p' of three Greek words, pistin paraschon and pasin in verse 31.

Reactions for and against

v.32-34 The Athenian guffaws are particularly inept in that they do not appreciate that Paul is making a direct challenge to that classic Athenian tragedy, the Eumenides, line 648, 'Of a person once dead there is no resurrection'.

We do not know who Dionysius the Areopagite or Damaris were. Various mystical writings were later falsely attributed to Dionysius, and he was even identified with the first Bishop of Paris. It is worth noting that Luke is always careful to give women the same importance as men. Again and again in his gospel women and men are paired: Zechariah and Mary, Simeon and Anna, the man who finds the lost sheep and the woman who finds the lost coin, and many others. Women certainly played an important and honoured part in early Christianity.

Women played a significant role in Paul's apostolate. In Acts 16:14 Lydia was converted to be the first Christian in Europe. Priscilla was an important catechist, first mentioned in Acts 18:2, and also in Romans 16. The First Letter to the Corinthians was written in answer to Chloe's delegation (1 Corinthians 1:11). The Letter to the Romans was carried by Phoebe (Romans 16:1). Junia is described as 'prominent' among the apostles in Rome (Romans 16:7). Women played a part in public worship (1 Corinthians 11:5).

The Word Lives On

This brilliant piece of writing is too succinct and artistic for easy reading. It is included in the Lectionary only for Wednesday of the sixth week of Easter.

The sixth preface for Sundays in Ordinary Time alludes to Paul's speech in Athens when it reads: 'In you we live and move and have our being. Each day you show us a Father's love.'

Acropolis, Athens, Greece.

Live the Word of God

Listen again to the reading: Acts 17:16-34

Suggestions for reflection and prayer

Paul affirms that we can get to know God through the natural creation we see all around us.

❖ What is to you the most potent evidence of God in creation? Flowers? The seasons? The wonder of life itself? The complexity of the human being? Love? Conscience?

❖ Would you say that the ability to see God in creation is the chief glory of human beings?

❖ What is the chief value that revelation gives you above the God of the philosophers?

The complacency of the Athenians is not unlike that of many educated and uneducated non-believers today, who simply do not feel the need for belief or religion.

❖ Do I ever find myself in this situation, and what is the answer to it?

❖ What can I do to help such people?

❖ What is the difference between religion and superstition?

The Second Vatican Council teaches: God is not far distant from those who in shadows and images seek the unknown God, for God gives to all life and breath and all things, and as Saviour wills that all be saved. Those also can attain to salvation who through no fault of their own do not know the Gospel of Christ or his Church, yet sincerely seek God and moved by grace strive by their deeds to do his will as it is known to them through the dictates of conscience. (Lumen Gentium 16)

Sculpture on St Peter's basilica door : Vatican II council.

The Foundation of
the Church at Corinth

Hear the Word of God

Read Acts 18:1-17

After this Paul left Athens and went to Corinth. [2] There he found a Jew named Aquila, a native of Pontus, who had recently come from Italy with his wife Priscilla, because Claudius had ordered all Jews to leave Rome. Paul went to see them, [3] and, because he was of the same trade, he stayed with them, and they worked together—by trade they were tentmakers. [4] Every sabbath he would argue in the synagogue and would try to convince Jews and Greeks.

[5] When Silas and Timothy arrived from Macedonia, Paul was occupied with proclaiming the word, testifying to the Jews that the Messiah was Jesus. [6] When they opposed and reviled him, in protest he shook the dust from his clothes and said to them, 'Your blood be on your own heads! I am innocent. From now on I will go to the Gentiles.' [7] Then he left the synagogue and went to the house of a man named Titius Justus, a worshipper of God; his house was next door to the synagogue. [8] Crispus, the official of the synagogue, became a believer in the Lord, together with all his household; and many of the Corinthians who heard Paul became believers and were baptized. [9] One night the Lord said to Paul in a vision, 'Do not be afraid, but speak and do not be silent; [10] for I am with you, and no one will lay a hand on you to harm you, for there are many in this city who are my people.' [11] He stayed there for a year and six months, teaching the word of God among them.

[12] But when Gallio was proconsul of Achaia, the Jews made a united attack on Paul and brought him before the tribunal. [13] They said, 'This man is persuading people to worship God in ways that are contrary to the law.' [14] Just as Paul was about to speak, Gallio said to the Jews, 'If it were a matter of crime or serious villainy, I would be justified in accepting the complaint of you Jews; [15] but since it is a matter of questions about words and names and your own law, see to it yourselves; I do not wish to be a judge of these matters.' [16] And he dismissed them from the tribunal. [17] Then all of them seized Sosthenes, the official of the synagogue, and beat him in front of the tribunal. But Gallio paid no attention to any of these things.

Opposite: Tentmaking of Paul, Priscilla and Aquila.

Understand the Word of God

This session will explore:

- ❖ the establishment of the Corinthian community
- ❖ the expulsion of Jews from Rome under Claudius
- ❖ the proclamation of Jesus as the Messiah or the Christ
- ❖ the three occasions when Paul is repulsed by the Jews and turns to the Gentiles

Setting in the Book

This is a significant stage in the progress of Paul's mission. He seems to have worked from a series of mission centres. His original commission took place, of course, at Antioch in Syria. In the opening verses of Acts chapter 13 Barnabas and Paul are sent out at the instigation of the Holy Spirit on what becomes known as the first missionary journey of Paul. Paul returned to Syrian Antioch periodically, at the end of each of his journeys, as is clear from Acts 14:26 and 18:22.

Paul also had a mission centre in Greece at Corinth. He stayed there initially for eighteen months (*verse 11*), but returned there on other occasions. In Asia Minor (modern Turkey) his centre was Ephesus, where he stayed for over two years (*Acts 19:10*), and to whose elders he gave a special parting message (*Acts 20:17-36*). Finally Paul seems to have wanted to establish a centre for the western Mediterranean in Rome, which would furnish a supply-line for his mission to Spain in the far West (*Romans 15:23-24*).

There are two Antiochs visited by Paul in Acts, one in Syria, the other in Pisidia in southern Turkey. Both cities were founded about 300 BC by the Hellenistic king, Seleucus, in honour of his father Antiochus. A number of other cities of that name also existed.

Corinth is a city straddling the isthmus which joins the Peloponnese to northern Greece. Its wealth was founded on its double port, one facing east, one facing west. Before the Corinthian canal was gouged out, shipping avoided braving the dangerous currents and rocks of the south coast of the Peloponnese by unloading their cargo in one port, dragging it across the isthmus on a sort of trolley-path, and reloading on the other side. It was also the centre for the famous biennial Isthmian Games (more popular and more prestigious than the neighbouring Olympic Games). In ancient times it enjoyed a somewhat dubious reputation as a sort of Las Vegas of Greece.

The two letters of Paul to Corinth which we have, and the references to other letters which have not survived, make it amply clear that leadership and guidance of this community was a challenge to Paul. In the Acts of the Apostles Luke does not see it as his business to highlight the flaws and tensions in the fledgling Church, so leaves all this unsaid. In any case, it took time for the community to be formed, and the letters to the Corinthians reflect the situation when the community had been in existence for some time. The tensions he does mention are uniquely those between Paul and those Jews who resisted the message of Christ.

What Kind of Text?

This narrative passage falls into three parts. Paul's initial settlement in Corinth and his missionary preaching is reported in verses 1-4. His formal response to his rejection by the Jews is found in verses 5-10. The court scene in verses 11-17 is a favourite set topic for Acts and for similar literary pieces of the time.

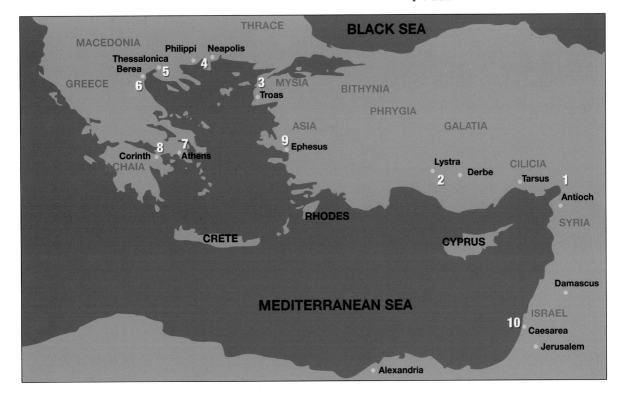

Second Missionary Journey of Paul.

Commentary: verse by verse reading

Paul arrives in Corinth

vv.1-2 Despite some conversions, Paul's visit to Athens does not seem to have been a success. His strictures in 1 Corinthians 1:17-25 on the folly of human wisdom may reflect his dissatisfaction with this experience.

1 Corinthians 16:19 The churches of Asia send greetings. Aquila and Prisca, together with the church in their house, greet you warmly in the Lord.

Romans 16:3 Greet Prisca and Aquila, who work with me in Christ Jesus.

The husband-and-wife catechetical partnership of Aquila and Priscilla (Prisca) played an active peripatetic part in Paul's apostolate. They reappear later, living at Ephesus (*1 Corinthians 16:19*), and then again back in Rome (*Romans 16:3*).

The decree of expulsion of Jews from Rome is an intriguing puzzle. It is mentioned by the Roman writer Suetonius under the year 49/50, as a consequence of a riot *impulsore Chresto*, which should mean 'instigated by Chrestus'. Suetonius does not say that all Jews were expelled from Rome, an unlikely mass movement, since there were many thousand Jews in Rome at this stage. 'Chrestus', a frequent slave-name, meaning 'useful', would be pronounced exactly as 'Christus', which could have caused confusion in one who had heard only remotely of Jesus the Christ.

Temple of Apollo, Corinth, Greece.

Quite possibly there was in one or a few synagogues a disagreement between those who accepted or rejected Christ, which attracted enough notice to deserve action and mention by the historian. However, the edict was soon cancelled or disregarded, possibly at the death of Claudius in 54, for Priscilla and Aquila were back in Rome in the early 50s.

vv. 3-4 Paul was, of course, a Pharisee, but this by no means excludes being a simple artisan such as a tent-maker. Pharisaism was a distinction of legal observance rather than class, and many Pharisees were simple, even impoverished, trades-people. Paul several times insists that he made his own living and refused to be a burden on anyone. He accepted monetary gifts only from his special friends, the Philippians (*Philippians 4:10-18*). At this time tents were made from skins rather than canvas, so that itinerants like Paul and his hosts at Corinth needed to carry for their trade only needle, thread and a scraping-knife.

Paul's response to the Jews

v.5 In the preaching to the Jews the point to be emphasised was always that Jesus was the Messiah or the Christ. For us Christians this is easy and obvious, but for the Jews of the time there were many different concepts of God's messianic plan.

The principal object for the Jews – and for Jesus himself – was not so much the person of the Messiah as the fact of the Kingdom of God, God's sovereignty over the world being renewed and fulfilled. This could be seen as the coming of God, the final visitation of God, transforming history. This coming was often, but not always, seen in terms of the anointed kingship of David's line. Nor was it clear whether the final coming was the coming of God or of God's messenger.

A further difficulty was that the world had not yet come to an end, and was not the coming of God the climax and conclusion of history? Furthermore, was not God's kingdom the elimination of all suffering and distress, a total joy and happiness? Had this really come to pass?

Suetonius writes as follows in his account of the emperor Claudius: Since the Jews constantly made disturbances at the instigation of Chrestus, he expelled them from Rome.
(Claudius 25)

St Bede comments on Paul the tent-maker: Symbolically, Peter the fisherman drew us from the waves of the world by the nets of faith. Similarly Paul, by his deeds and by his words, set up a tent of protection against the rains of sin, against the heat of temptation and against the gales of snares.
(Commentary on Acts, c. 18)

So Paul had a good deal of explaining to do! All this could be put in perspective only by a full understanding of the significance of the Resurrection.

v.6 Now occurs the second of three occasions when Paul formally declares that the Jewish refusal has forced him to turn to the Gentiles. Luke is careful to show that God has not reneged on his promises to the Jews. These promises were fulfilled, in that in each place Jews are converted. It is only through the stubbornness of other Jews that Paul is forced to turn to the Gentiles.

St John Chrysostom writes: When they opposed and reviled him, he shook out his garments and said, "Your blood be upon your heads!" He does this to frighten them not only with words but also with action. And he argues rather vehemently because he has already persuaded many of them. "I am innocent," he says. "From now on I will go to the Gentiles." So we too are accountable for the blood of those entrusted to us, if we neglect them. (Homilies on the Acts, 39)

Corinth: The Richest City of Them All.

The saying about their blood being on their own heads refers back to Deuteronomy 21:6-7. If the elders of a community have done their best and failed to discover the culprit of a murder, they are to wash their hands with this saying to affirm their own clearance from blood-guilt. Pilate does the same at the trial of Jesus (Matthew 27:24).

The first of the three occasions in which Paul turns to the Gentiles was at Antioch in Pisidia and is narrated in 13:51, the last occasion will be in Rome (*28:25-28*), so that of the three occasions one is in Asia, one in Greece and one at the heart of the Empire. On each occasion Paul makes a biblical gesture and confirms it with a biblical saying. Here he shakes out his cloak, just as at Antioch he shook the dust off his feet.

vv.7-11 When Paul turns to the Gentiles at Corinth he has greater success. Crispus and Justus are obviously Gentile names. In his eighteen-month stay Paul has time to form the community which will later cause him so much trouble. Nevertheless, it is reassuring that Paul was granted a special booster-vision to encourage him at this difficult time (*verses 9-10*). He must have had moments of disappointment at his failures, just like anyone else. The Lord looks after his workers!

The words of the vision echo the promise of the support of the Spirit given in Luke 12:11-12: 'when they bring you before the synagogues, the rulers, and the authorities, do not worry about how you are to defend yourselves or what you are to say'. Immediately after this encouragement Paul will be taken before magistrates and authorities, but will not need to think out how to defend himself.

The trial scene

vv.12-17 The incident ends with the sort of scene so beloved of Hellenistic writers, a court-scene and a riot burlesqued. Gallio is a good deal more sage than was Pontius Pilate. This is not surprising, for Gallio came from a senatorial family which had generations of experience of dealing with awkward matters, and he knew that he was out of his depth in matters of Jewish legal disputes. At least, that is how he interprets the charge.

The accusers do not get a chance to explain which 'law' Paul is supposed to have contravened, Roman or Jewish. It could be the Roman law, claiming that Jesus, not the Emperor, was the Lord. If it was a Jewish law, Gallio was not only right but wise to refuse to get embroiled in the complexities of Jewish Law. Pilate had been less circumspect.

The mention of Gallio gives us our only firm date in the Acts. A chance inscription at Delphi sets his year of office in 51 AD. He was brother of the philosopher Seneca, who tells us that he was a hypochondriac and did not complete his year of office, fleeing from Greece before the summer heat became too intense.

It is intriguing to wonder whether Sosthenes, who was president of the synagogue, became a Christian and is the Sosthenes mentioned by Paul in 1 Corinthians 1:1. In this case he must have followed Paul to Ephesus, where the letter was written.

We read in the Catechism of the Catholic Church: The Church is nothing other than "the family of God". From the beginning, the core of the Church was often constituted by those who had become believers "together with all their household". These families who became believers were islands of Christian life in an unbelieving world. (1655)

St John Chrysostom writes:

Let us also imitate Sosthenes: to them that beat us, let us return blow for blow, by meekness, by silence, by long-suffering. You, a human being, insult your fellow man? You, a servant, your fellow servant? But why do I wonder at this, when many even insult God? To endure when insulted is God's part; to be merely abusive is the part of the devil. (Homilies on the Acts 39)

The Word Lives On

This passage is read on Thursday of the sixth week of Easter, in the course of the Easter-time journey through the story of the early Church.

Ancient writers took an interest in this passage because with its reference to Paul working as a tent-maker it gives an idea of the importance of manual work. St John Chrysostom wrote: 'Let no one who is a craftsman be ashamed, but rather those who are reared for no purpose and do nothing, the ones who employ many servants and enjoy an immense court.' (Catena on the *Acts of the Apostles, 18.3*)

Blessed John Paul II wrote in his encyclical on work, Laborem Exercens, *written in 1981: The teaching of Christ on work, based on the example of his life during his years in Nazareth, finds a particularly lively echo in the teaching of the Apostle Paul. Paul boasts of working at his trade (he was probably a tent-maker, Acts 18:3), and thanks to that work he was able even as an Apostle to earn his own bread (Acts 20:34-35). (26)*

Live the Word of God

Listen again to the reading: Acts 18:1-17

Suggestions for reflection and prayer

How is it that some people refuse the message of Christ and some accept it?

❖ Does not God love all people equally?

❖ I have been given the chance to respond to Christ's invitation. Have I adequately done so?

The community at Corinth to which Paul wrote had all kinds of difficulties.

❖ How is the Spirit at work in the Christian community to which I belong?

❖ What are the gifts at work in those around me?

❖ Do I make generous and willing use of the gifts by which I could help others and contribute to the wellbeing of the community?

In 1990 Blessed John Paul II wrote in Redemptoris Missio, his encyclical on the missionary activity of the church: It is precisely because he is "sent" that the missionary experiences the consoling presence of Christ, who is with him at every moment of life - "Do not be afraid...for I am with you" (Acts 18:9-10) - and who awaits him in the heart of every person. (88)

The Riot at Ephesus

Hear the Word of God

Read Acts 19:23-40

²³ About that time no little disturbance broke out concerning the Way. ²⁴ A man named Demetrius, a silversmith who made silver shrines of Artemis, brought no little business to the artisans. ²⁵ These he gathered together, with the workers of the same trade, and said, 'Men, you know that we get our wealth from this business. ²⁶ You also see and hear that not only in Ephesus but in almost the whole of Asia this Paul has persuaded and drawn away a considerable number of people by saying that gods made with hands are not gods. ²⁷ And there is danger not only that this trade of ours may come into disrepute but also that the temple of the great goddess Artemis will be scorned, and she will be deprived of her majesty that brought all Asia and the world to worship her.'

²⁸ When they heard this, they were enraged and shouted, 'Great is Artemis of the Ephesians!' ²⁹ The city was filled with the confusion; and people rushed together to the theatre, dragging with them Gaius and Aristarchus, Macedonians who were Paul's travelling-companions. ³⁰ Paul wished to go into the crowd, but the disciples would not let him; ³¹ even some officials of the province of Asia, who were friendly to him, sent him a message urging him not to venture into the theatre.

³² Meanwhile, some were shouting one thing, some another; for the assembly was in confusion, and most of them did not know why they had come together. ³³ Some of the crowd gave instructions to Alexander, whom the Jews had pushed forward. And Alexander motioned for silence and tried to make a defence before the people. ³⁴ But when they recognized that he was a Jew, for about two hours all of them shouted in unison, 'Great is Artemis of the Ephesians!' ³⁵ But when the town clerk had quietened the crowd, he said, 'Citizens of Ephesus, who is there that does not know that the city of the Ephesians is the temple-keeper of the great Artemis and of the statue that fell from heaven? ³⁶ Since these things cannot be denied, you ought to be quiet and do nothing rash. ³⁷ You have brought these men here who are neither temple-robbers nor blasphemers of our goddess. ³⁸ If therefore Demetrius and the artisans with him have a complaint against anyone, the courts are open, and there are proconsuls; let them bring charges there against one another. ³⁹ If there is anything further you want to know, it must be settled in the regular assembly. ⁴⁰ For we are in danger of being charged with rioting today, since there is no cause that we can give to justify this commotion.'

Opposite: St Paul Preaching Before the Temple of Diana at Ephesus, by Adolf Pirsch.

Understand the Word of God

This session will explore:

❖ the situation of the Church at Ephesus

❖ the challenge for Christians presented by the imperial cult

❖ Luke's skill and care for accuracy of detail

❖ a possible imprisonment of Paul at Ephesus

Setting in the Book

Ephesus was the capital of the province of Asia, and home to a major temple of Rome and Augustus, so a major centre of the imperial cult which united the Roman provinces of the East. By this time, at any rate in the East, the Emperor was considered a god, and was paid divine honours in temples.

Paul's stay of over two years at Ephesus represents the last major incident and the last foundation of a Church before he sets off for Jerusalem and his final captivity (or at least the last recounted in Acts). Situated on the Aegean coast at the mouth of the River Meander, Ephesus was one of the greatest cities of the time, ranked with Rome and Alexandria, certainly the most splendid city in the Roman province of Asia and its administrative capital. Today its reconstructed buildings are perhaps the most impressive of any city of the ancient East. The temple of Artemis was the largest temple in the Roman world and counted as one of the Seven Wonders of the World. Its platform covers 100,000 square feet.

It is surprising that the cult of the Emperor is mentioned in the account in Acts only obliquely. The 'officials of the province of Asia', also known as 'Asiarchs' *(verse 31)* were the priests of the cult. As we have seen, Luke is anxious to minimise any clash between Christianity and the Roman authorities, so makes no mention of the rivalry of the imperial cult at this important centre.

By the time the Book of Revelation comes to be written the imperial cult was the great rival for the loyalty of Christians. In that book it is represented as the Beast and the great Dragon, 'the primeval serpent', persecuting Christians and drawing them away from their loyalty to Christ, attempting to swallow the Child of the Woman as soon as it is born (Revelation 12).

This was not Paul's first visit to Ephesus. He had made a brief visit after the affair at Corinth. He had been well received by the Jews, and left the husband-and-wife team of catechists, Priscilla and Aquila, there *(18:18-21)*. The somewhat mysterious figure of Apollos, an Alexandrian Jew, had also preached fearlessly there, at the same time as completing his own instruction from Priscilla and Aquila *(18:24-26)*.

This is, however, Paul's first seriously long stay at Ephesus, and he must have set up the community organization on this occasion.

Luke's account of Paul's stay comprises various incidents. It begins with Paul's meeting with the disciples of John the Baptist (*19:1-7*). This mysterious group had never even heard of the Holy Spirit, having been baptized only with John's baptism of repentance. Paul instructs them more fully, baptizes them, and they receive the Spirit, speaking in tongues and prophesying. Paul's proclamation of the kingdom of God follows (*19:8*). As usual he began his proclamation in the synagogue, but, again as usual, after three months it became clear that the Jews would not accept the message, and Paul moved to the lecture room of Tyrannus, where he preached with success for two years to both Jews and Greeks (*19:9-10*). So some Jews, at least, accepted the message.

There follows a nice little burlesque about Paul's triumph over the spirits (*19:13-17*). Such competition with the spirits and magic is a regular feature of Acts, for there was obviously a good deal of superstition and trust in magic in the eastern Mediterranean at the time. The riot which follows is the subject of our reading.

In the verses immediately preceding our passage, Luke makes it very clear that Paul's enthusiasm for his preaching ministry is undimmed. We read in verse 21: Paul resolved in the Spirit to go through Macedonia and Achaia, and then go on to Jerusalem. He said: After I have gone there, I must also see Rome. For the present, however, Paul stayed for some time longer in Asia (verse 22).

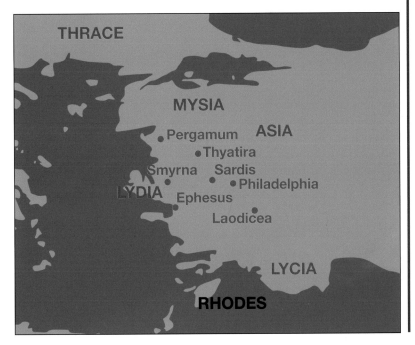

The seven churches of the book of Revelation.

What Kind of Text?

Contemporary audiences clearly enjoyed a little mild violence, just as a previous generation to ours enjoyed the slapstick of comedy and a modern audience the knock-about of gangster films. We have already met it in the scene before Gallio at Corinth (*18:17*), and will meet it again in the attempt to lynch Paul in the Temple at Jerusalem (*21:30-31*).

Such scenes are a regular feature of first-century junk-novels such as *Chaereas and Callirhoe*. Luke is aware of the historian's duty, as Quintilian put it, to entertain as well as to edify. This does not, of course, mean that Luke invented the scene, but only that he wrote it up, making much of a comparatively minor incident in order to entertain his readers. Such details as we can check are strikingly accurate, as we shall see.

The ancient Greek novel called Chaereas and Callirhoe was written by Chariton of Aphrodisias. Fragments of the text on papyri suggest it was written in the middle of the first century AD. It is the oldest surviving ancient novel, a love story set in 400 BC Syracuse.

Quintilian lived in the first century. He was born in Spain, but travelled to Rome and became an expert on rhetoric, the art of speaking.

Temple of Artemis: Considered one of the seven wonders of the ancient world, Ephesus' Temple of Artemis was dedicated to the goddess of the hunt. Only the foundation and one column remains of this temple which once measured 425 ft long, 220 ft wide and 60 ft high.

Commentary: verse by verse reading

Disquiet in Ephesus

vv.23-24 Diana (or Artemis) of Ephesus was a popular goddess, and presumably the silver statuettes were a tourist attraction. None of the silver statues have survived. No doubt at some stage over the centuries they were melted down and used for coinage or other silver objects, for valuable metal is often re-used in this way. On the other hand a number of stone statues of Diana of Ephesus have survived – they cannot be reused for other purposes! The statues leave no doubt that, besides being goddess of hunting, she was also a fertility mother-goddess. Fertility of animals, but especially of humans, was always a worry in the ancient world, limited as it was in the science of genetics.

vv.25-27 The silversmith Demetrius is surely overplaying his hand in suggesting that Paul's conversions to Christianity threatened to reduce the cult of Diana to unimportance, but he could have been over-reacting to some trivial incident. As anyone who has been involuntarily caught up in a demonstration can testify, crowds are notoriously volatile, and often not quite sure what they are demonstrating about.

Cult statue from Ephesus called the "Great Artemis" (2nd cent. AD).

Other references to Christianity as 'the Way' in Acts:

9:2 If Saul found any who belonged to the Way, he would bring them bound to Jerusalem.

19:9 When some spoke evil of the Way before the congregation, Paul left them.

22:4 Paul said: 'I persecuted this Way up to the point of death by binding both men and women and putting them in prison.'

24:14 Paul said: 'But this I admit to you, that according to the Way, which they call a sect, I worship the God of our ancestors.'

24:22 Felix was rather well informed about the Way.

The statement that 'gods made with hands are not gods' echoes what Paul said in Athens: The God who made the world and everything in it, he who is Lord of heaven and earth, does not live in shrines made by human hands. (Acts 17:24) He continued: We ought not to think that the deity is like gold, or silver, or stone, an image formed by the art and imagination of mortals. (17:29)

The Riot

vv.28-29 The riot begins with the cry 'Great is Artemis of the Ephesians!', which is repeated in verse 34 and kept up for two hours. The great theatre at Ephesus still exists, built into the hill facing the sea which forms the backdrop of the city. It has seating for 25,000 people, and is known to have been the regular place for the citizens' assembly and discussion.

vv.30-31 It is obviously dangerous for Paul to try to address the crowd. The local officials give him good advice. The name 'Asiarchs' (Greek *Asiarchai*), translated here as 'officials of the province of Asia', suggests 'rulers of Asia', whereas in fact these officials were in charge only of the cult of Rome and Augustus which bound the province of Asia together. However, the important factor is that Luke gets their title right. Unlikely though it may be that Paul the leather-worker had personal friends among such high officials, Luke is fond of showing the notice which Christianity attracted among important people.

vv. 32-36 The chief magistrate of the city, who takes charge of the situation and eventually brings it under control in verse 35, had in fact the title *grammateus* or town clerk.

This is also the case with the proconsul of Cyprus, Sergius Paulus, in 13:6-12. The proconsul witnesses how Paul deals with the magician Elymas, bringing temporary blindness upon him when he tries to turn the proconsul away from the faith. When the proconsul saw what had happened, he believed, for he was astonished at the teaching about the Lord. (Acts 13:12)

St John Chrysostom comments on this passage: Such is the way of crowds, to jump to conclusions and become enraged on any pretext. That is why one must do everything after careful consideration. "Some cried one thing, some another." For such is the behaviour of the crowd. It simply follows, as when fire alights on wood. (Homilies on Acts, 42)

The Theatre at Ephesus.

vv.37-40 The town clerk is realistically presented as concerned about the possible charge of *stasis*, riot or rebellion (*verse 40*), which might incur the wrath of the Roman authorities. Rebellion was always a possibility among the subject peoples of the Empire, and illegal or irregular assembly, which could constitute a beginning of this, was forbidden. Hence any complaints must wait for a properly constituted assembly (*verse 39*).

It all seems to have ended quietly, but there is some question whether Luke is telling the whole truth about Paul's stay at Ephesus. Luke, in 19:10, says that he stayed in Ephesus for more than two years, yet he hardly gives us a programme large enough to fill that time. Paul was an energetic sort of person!

Writing to the Corinthians Paul tells of 'the affliction we experienced in Asia'. He says 'we were so utterly, unbearably crushed that we despaired of life itself. Indeed, we felt that we had received the sentence of death so that we would rely not on ourselves but on God who raises the dead.' *(2 Corinthians 1:8-9)*. Did Paul spend some part of those two years in detention?

The town clerk tells the crowd to resort to the courts and to the proconsul. The proconsul, who would formerly have been consul in Rome, was the provincial governor and would have resided in Ephesus, since it was the capital of the province of Asia.

Paul writes to the Philippians: It has become known throughout the whole imperial guard (whole praetorium) and to everyone else that my imprisonment is for Christ. (1:13) If he is referring to imprisonment in Ephesus, 'the praetorium' would be the governor's guard, for the governor would have been a praetor or pro-praetor. We can only speculate.

The Library of Celsus at Ephesus.

The Word Lives On

This particular word does not seem to live on anywhere in the readings prescribed for the liturgy! However, anyone who has visited Ephesus and its theatre cannot but remember this incident.

Saint Paul preaching at Ephesus, by Eustache Le Sueur. This painting relates to Acts 19:9 which tells of new converts in Ephesus who had practised magic, burning their books. Their value was calculated at 50,000 silver pieces.

Live the Word of God

In his encyclical Redemptoris Missio of 1990 Blessed John Paul II wrote: The missionaries continued along this path, taking into account people's hopes and expectations, their anguish and sufferings, as well as their culture, in order to proclaim to them salvation in Christ. If they are to recognize the true God, they must abandon the false gods which they themselves have made and open themselves to the One whom God has sent to remedy their ignorance and satisfy the longings of their hearts. Under the impulse of the Spirit, the Christian faith is decisively opened to the nations. Witness to Christ spreads to the most important centers of the eastern Mediterranean and then to Rome and the far regions of the West. It is the Spirit who is the source of the drive to press on, not only geographically but also beyond the frontiers of race and religion, for a truly universal mission. (25)

Listen again to the reading: Acts 19:23-40.

Here we see the pressures of public opinion at their most ugly, manipulated for the sake of one particular position in an attempt to crush a minority opinion.

✤ Do I do enough to inform my own views and my own conscience on the important political and moral issues of the day?

✤ Do I dare to defend Christian positions in public or in conversation with those who fail to appreciate them? Do I reflect on, or even take part in, public debates in the media or elsewhere?

✤ What can I do to prevent such warping of public favour, to defend unpopular positions which are nevertheless binding on Christians?

The imperial cult involved saying 'The Emperor is Lord' and denying 'Christ is Lord'. Christians would have been considered stubbornly partisan, ignorant and stuck in a backwater for this attitude, just as Christians are today in many circles.

✤ Do I build my life and my estimate of others on a material scale of values?

✤ Do I hold my own as my conscience dictates?

✤ Do I help others to hold their own?

✤ Or do I shrink into silence and quietly paddle my canoe further up the backwater?

Paul in Jerusalem

Hear the Word of God

Read Acts 21:17-39

[17] When we arrived in Jerusalem, the brothers welcomed us warmly. [18] The next day Paul went with us to visit James; and all the elders were present. [19] After greeting them, he related one by one the things that God had done among the Gentiles through his ministry. [20] When they heard it, they praised God. Then they said to him, 'You see, brother, how many thousands of believers there are among the Jews, and they are all zealous for the law. [21] They have been told about you that you teach all the Jews living among the Gentiles to forsake Moses, and that you tell them not to circumcise their children or observe the customs. [22] What then is to be done? They will certainly hear that you have come. [23] So do what we tell you. We have four men who are under a vow. [24] Join these men, go through the rite of purification with them, and pay for the shaving of their heads. Thus all will know that there is nothing in what they have been told about you, but that you yourself observe and guard the law. [25] But as for the Gentiles who have become believers, we have sent a letter with our judgement that they should abstain from what has been sacrificed to idols and from blood and from what is strangled and from fornication.' [26] Then Paul took the men, and the next day, having purified himself, he entered the temple with them, making public the completion of the days of purification when the sacrifice would be made for each of them.

[27] When the seven days were almost completed, the Jews from Asia, who had seen him in the temple, stirred up the whole crowd. They seized him, [28] shouting, 'Fellow-Israelites, help! This is the man who is teaching everyone everywhere against our people, our law, and this place; more than that, he has actually brought Greeks into the temple and has defiled this holy place.' [29] For they had previously seen Trophimus the Ephesian with him in the city, and they supposed that Paul had brought him into the temple. [30] Then all the city was aroused, and the people rushed together. They seized Paul and dragged him out of the temple, and immediately the doors were shut. [31] While they were trying to kill him, word came to the tribune of the cohort that all Jerusalem was in an uproar. [32] Immediately he took soldiers and centurions and ran down to them. When they saw the tribune and the soldiers, they stopped beating Paul. [33] Then the tribune came, arrested him, and ordered him to be bound with two chains; he inquired who he was and what he had done. [34] Some in the crowd shouted one thing, some another; and as he could not learn the facts because of the uproar, he ordered him to be brought into the barracks. [35] When Paul came to the steps, the violence of the mob was so great that he had to be carried by the soldiers. [36] The crowd that followed kept shouting, 'Away with him!'

[37] Just as Paul was about to be brought into the barracks, he said to the tribune, 'May I say something to you?' The tribune replied, 'Do you know Greek? [38] Then you are not the Egyptian who recently stirred up a revolt and led the four thousand assassins out into the wilderness?' [39] Paul replied, 'I am a Jew, from Tarsus in Cilicia, a citizen of an important city; I beg you, let me speak to the people.'

Understand the Word of God

This session will explore:

❖ the 'we-passages' in Acts

❖ the persistent problem of observance of the Jewish Law by Christians

❖ Paul's Roman citizenship

Setting in the Book

A pall of sadness hangs over this section of the book, for it is made clear at every step that Paul is on his way to imprisonment. He has taken his last farewell of the elders of Ephesus with a great final speech of encouragement (*20:18-35*), the form of which was typical of Hellenistic farewell speeches by a great leader, preparing his followers for his death or departure. In content it was very reminiscent of Jesus' own warnings to his disciples that there would be persecution and false teachers in the Church, but that the presence of the Holy Spirit would strengthen them. On Paul's journey to Jerusalem Agabus has acted out a prophecy of the imprisonment by tying up his hands and feet with Paul's belt (*21:11*), and so Paul arrives in Jerusalem.

What was Paul's purpose in going there? Firstly, it is clear from the Letter to the Galatians chapters 1-2 that, despite his divine warrant as apostle (*Galatians 1:1*), Paul saw it as important to maintain contact with the mother-Church at Jerusalem. This may be the reason why Luke so insistently regards Jerusalem as the pivotal point in the Gospel and the Acts: the Gospel begins in Jerusalem and ends in Jerusalem, and it is from Jerusalem that the faith spreads to 'the ends of the earth' in Acts. Luke sees Jerusalem as the guarantee of the unity of the Church which he so treasures.

Acts 21:11 Agabus came to us and took Paul's belt, bound his own feet and hands with it, and said, 'Thus says the Holy Spirit, "This is the way the Jews in Jerusalem will bind the man who owns this belt and will hand him over to the Gentiles."'

Galatians 1:1 Paul an apostle – sent neither by human commission nor from human authorities, but through Jesus Christ and God the Father, who raised him from the dead.

Page 102: The Apostle Paul in Prison, by Rembrandt.

There is, however, another weighty reason for Paul's return to Jerusalem now at this point. In his letters, especially Romans 15:25-26 and 2 Corinthians chapters 8-9, he expresses his concern about a great collection for the poor of Jerusalem. This seems to be an act of recognition and a tribute from the Gentile Churches to the mother-Church, acknowledging their debt to the base community. There may well be more significance than that. After Paul's row with Peter at Antioch, narrated in Galatians 2:11, and his great split from the Hebraists Barnabas and John Mark, which is reported in Acts 15:36-39, the collection may well be a way of eventually healing the wound. A fat cheque is often useful in assuaging hurt feelings!

What Kind of Text?

It happens that this is the first time we have encountered a 'we-passage'. This is the name given to certain passages in Acts recounted not in the third person, but in the first person plural, indicating that the author of the text was one of those involved. The first of these occurs, in some manuscripts only, at 11:27, which would suggest that Luke joined Paul at Antioch at the end of his first journey. The second begins at 16:10, when Paul crosses to Europe for the first time. It would suggest that the author was with Paul at Philippi, from where he comes to join Paul again in 20:6, and accompanies him as far as Jerusalem. The final 'we-passage' begins at 27:1, and shows the author accompanying Paul from Caesarea to Rome.

Many of the details of these sections are concerned with travel arrangements, and it is almost as though the author had kept a travel diary to provide useful details of lengths of voyage and routes for a future occasion. For us, however, the principal asset of these passages is that they show that Luke was a companion of Paul, and could presumably have informed himself about the details of his travels and his concerns. Scholars have claimed that such first-person narratives are a convention for sea voyages and do not imply the author's presence, but the texts they quote do not bear this out.

Galatians 2:11 But when Cephas (Peter) came to Antioch, I opposed him to his face, because he stood self-condemned.

Acts 15:36-39 After some days Paul said to Barnabas, 'Come let us return and visit the believers in every city where we proclaimed the word of the Lord and see how they are doing.' Barnabas wanted to take with them John called Mark. But Paul decided not to take with them one who had deserted them in Pamphylia and had not accompanied them in the work. The disagreement became so sharp that they parted company; Barnabas took Mark with him and sailed away to Cyprus.

Acts 16:10 When he had seen the vision, we immediately tried to cross over to Macedonia, being convinced that God had called us to proclaim the good news to them.

Acts 20:6 We sailed from Philippi after the days of Unleavened Bread, and in five days we joined Paul and his companions in Troas, where we stayed for seven days.

Acts 27:1 It was decided that we were to sail for Italy.

Commentary: verse by verse reading

Paul undertakes a vow

v.17 A warm welcome is given to Paul in Jerusalem, but things soon become definitely frosty.

vv.18-22 James and the elders give glory to God for Paul's work of conversion of the Gentiles, but point out that there is a distinct difficulty, the reputation that Paul has encouraged 'all the Jews living among the Gentiles' to abandon the practice of the Law.

vv.23 If Paul is to be acceptable in Jerusalem he must show that he still values Jewish practices by paying for expensive ceremonies in the temple. Not a word of thanks for the gift of the money from Paul's collection! Indeed, it is almost as if they refused the money until the filthy Gentile money had been laundered by use of some of it in the temple. In the interests of stressing Church unity it seems that Luke is telling us only half the story.

vv.24-26 The vow must be a nazirite vow. This was a temporary vow by which someone could dedicate himself to God for a time, during which he must not drink from alcohol or grapes, must not incur corpse-defilement even for immediate family members, and may not cut his hair. Perhaps as a slight conciliatory gesture, the elders repeat the provisions of the apostolic letter written at the Council of Jerusalem (*15:28-29*), calling on Gentile Christians to observe a minimal set of requirements.

At the end of the vow a sacrifice including two lambs and a ram is to be offered. Luke is possibly a little confused here about the nazirite regulations. There is nothing about purification and 'the seven days' (*verse 27*) in the relevant texts of Numbers chapter 6. Luke is certainly writing principally for Gentile Christians, and he may well have been a Gentile himself, though this is one of very few passages where his knowledge of Judaism seems to be imperfect.

Paul submissively sets about performing the task set for him. This cannot have been easy for him, with his views on the inefficacy of Jewish practices. It shows in practice, however, how far he will go for the sake of peace within the Church.

Paul is putting into effect his own instructions in 1 Corinthians 8:9-13 about the strong not scandalizing the consciences of the weak. At Corinth some Christians thought it wrong to eat meat contaminated by being sacrificed to idols. Paul replies that personally he thinks non-existent idols cannot bring contamination, but that he refrains from eating such meat in order not to scandalise these believers.

Jerusalem.

The attack on Paul

vv.27-36 Paul was spotted in the temple by some Jews from the province of Asia, who falsely accused him of bringing an uncircumcised Ephesian into the Temple, a crime punishable by death. A riot broke out – and Luke has a predeliction for riots - from which Paul is rescued only by the Roman soldiers stationed in the adjacent Fortress Antonia specifically for this purpose, to nip in the bud any disturbances in the temple. The military tribune was in charge of a cohort, a detachment of one thousand men.

vv.37-38 Paul quickly establishes a bond with the tribune by his educated Greek. The revolt in the desert led by 'the Egyptian' is mentioned also by Josephus. He promised his mob of followers that, in a repeat of Joshua's miracle at Jericho, they would see the walls of Jerusalem fall down, but they were quickly dispersed, though the leader escaped. It is quite unclear why the tribune identified Paul as this rebel leader. The *sicarioi* ('dagger-men' translated here as 'assassins') is another name for the Zealots, the militants determined to expel the Romans. Their activities escalated during these years, and will eventually explode into the revolt of 66AD.

In the 'Antiquities' of Josephus (Book XX) it is written: There came out of Egypt about this time to Jerusalem, one who said he was a prophet, and advised the multitude of the common people to go along with him to the Mount of Olives, as it was called, which lay over against the city, and at a distance of five furlongs (one kilometre). He said further that he would show them from hence, how, at his command the walls of Jerusalem would fall down, and he promised that he would procure them an entrance into the city through those walls, when they had fallen down. Now when Felix (the governor) was informed of these things, he ordered his soldiers to take their weapons, and came against them with a great number of horsemen and footmen, from Jerusalem, and attacked the Egyptian and the people that were with him. He also slew 400 of them and took 200 alive. But the Egyptian himself escaped out of the fight, but did not appear any more. (20:169-172)

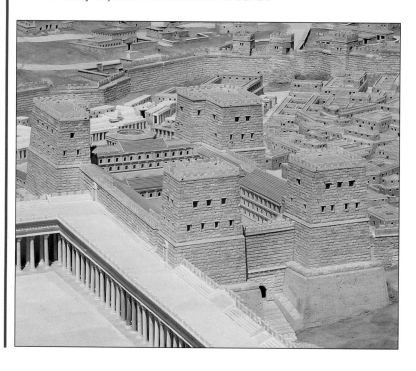

A model of the Antonia Fortress – currently in the Israel Museum, Jerusalem.

Paul Rescued, by Gustav Doré.

Paul's Roman citizenship is rather a puzzle. He never mentions it in his letters, and we can only guess how he came to have this highly-prized privilege – presumably from his family background in Tarsus. Some Jews are known to have enjoyed the privilege, but no known Pharisee is among them. Was acknowledgement of Caesar as Lord really compatible with Pharisaic loyalty to God as king? Paul's citizenship has, however, already served him at Philippi (16:37). It will also be the basis of the rest of the story of Acts, which revolves round his appeal to Rome.

v.39 Paul claims to be a Roman citizen. One of the most important consequences of citizenship was the right to a formal trial, so freedom from the summary justice inflicted on non-citizens. This is, of course, the secret of the trial of Jesus by Pilate: the governor did not have to adhere to any rules, but dispensed 'justice' to non-citizens, who had no rights, exactly as he saw fit. The penalties for a false claim to citizenship were dire, and citizens would carry a sort of passport, signed by ten fellow-citizens, to prove their rights.

The Word Lives On

This turning-point in Paul's story is not included in the readings prescribed for the liturgy. The truth is that the fifty days of the Easter season are not enough to enable a complete reading of the Acts of the Apostles, and the final chapters are quite inadequately covered.

St Paul (Upper Church, San Francesco, Assisi), by Giotto di Bondone

Live the Word of God

Listen again to the reading: Acts 21:17-39

Suggestions for reflection and prayer

Paul seems to be fully aware that he is heading for arrest and imprisonment at Jerusalem. He has already been exposed to the threat of death at Ephesus. His speech to the elders of Ephesus at Miletus shows that the Holy Spirit makes him aware that persecution awaits him. (See the extract from Acts 20 given on this page.) Paul has, however, no idea of the details.

Acts 20:22-23 Paul said: 'And now, as a captive to the Spirit, I am on my way to Jerusalem, not knowing what will happen to me there, except that the Holy Spirit testifies to me in every city that imprisonment and persecutions are waiting for me.'

✤ Is it true that 'the blood of martyrs is the seed of Christians' (Tertullian)?

✤ Which martyrs inspire me most?

✤ Would I have the courage to accept martyrdom for Christ?

✤ Am I truly committed to accepting what God sends me?

✤ What would I miss most if I were not a Christian?

Disunity in the Church has been a scandal since the earliest days, especially in view of Jesus' prayer for the unity of his followers in John 17. Differences of opinion and interpretation must exist, and even personal disagreements will require tolerance and forgiveness.

✤ How much difference must there be before I regard someone else as not a fellow-Christian?

✤ How much do I share with a non-Christian who believes in God under a different name?

✤ Is the unity of Christians a regular item in my own prayers?

✤ What else can I do to foster the unity for which Christ prayed?

The Shipwreck off Malta

Hear the Word of God

Read Acts 27:9-44

⁹ Since much time had been lost and sailing was now dangerous, because even the Fast had already gone by, Paul advised them, ¹⁰ saying, 'Sirs, I can see that the voyage will be with danger and much heavy loss, not only of the cargo and the ship, but also of our lives.' ¹¹ But the centurion paid more attention to the pilot and to the owner of the ship than to what Paul said. ¹² Since the harbour was not suitable for spending the winter, the majority was in favour of putting to sea from there, on the chance that somehow they could reach Phoenix, where they could spend the winter. It was a harbour of Crete, facing south-west and north-west.

¹³ When a moderate south wind began to blow, they thought they could achieve their purpose; so they weighed anchor and began to sail past Crete, close to the shore. ¹⁴ But soon a violent wind, called the northeaster, rushed down from Crete. ¹⁵ Since the ship was caught and could not be turned with its head to the wind, we gave way to it and were driven. ¹⁶ By running under the lee of a small island called Cauda we were scarcely able to get the ship's boat under control. ¹⁷ After hoisting it up they took measures to undergird the ship; then, fearing that they would run on the Syrtis, they lowered the sea-anchor and so were driven. ¹⁸ We were being pounded by the storm so violently that on the next day they began to throw the cargo overboard, ¹⁹ and on the third day with their own hands they threw the ship's tackle overboard. ²⁰ When neither sun nor stars appeared for many days, and no small tempest raged, all hope of our being saved was at last abandoned.

²¹ Since they had been without food for a long time, Paul then stood up among them and said, 'Men, you should have listened to me and not have set sail from Crete and thereby avoided this damage and loss. ²² I urge you now to keep up your courage, for there will be no loss of life among you, but only of the ship. ²³ For last night there stood by me an angel of the God to whom I belong and whom I worship, ²⁴ and he said, "Do not be afraid, Paul; you must stand before the emperor; and indeed, God has granted safety to all those who are sailing with you." ²⁵ So keep up your courage, men, for I have faith in God that it will be exactly as I have been told. ²⁶ But we will have to run aground on some island.'

Opposite: St Paul arriving at Malta, by Pieter Mulier the Younger.

27 When the fourteenth night had come, as we were drifting across the sea of Adria, about midnight the sailors suspected that they were nearing land. 28 So they took soundings and found twenty fathoms; a little farther on they took soundings again and found fifteen fathoms. 29 Fearing that we might run on the rocks, they let down four anchors from the stern and prayed for day to come. 30 But when the sailors tried to escape from the ship and had lowered the boat into the sea, on the pretext of putting out anchors from the bow, 31 Paul said to the centurion and the soldiers, 'Unless these men stay in the ship, you cannot be saved.' 32 Then the soldiers cut away the ropes of the boat and set it adrift.

33 Just before daybreak, Paul urged all of them to take some food, saying, 'Today is the fourteenth day that you have been in suspense and remaining without food, having eaten nothing. 34 Therefore I urge you to take some food, for it will help you survive; for none of you will lose a hair from your heads.' 35 After he had said this, he took bread; and giving thanks to God in the presence of all, he broke it and began to eat. 36 Then all of them were encouraged and took food for themselves. 37 (We were in all two hundred and seventy-six persons in the ship.) 38 After they had satisfied their hunger, they lightened the ship by throwing the wheat into the sea.

39 In the morning they did not recognize the land, but they noticed a bay with a beach, on which they planned to run the ship ashore, if they could. 40 So they cast off the anchors and left them in the sea. At the same time they loosened the ropes that tied the steering-oars; then hoisting the foresail to the wind, they made for the beach. 41 But striking a reef, they ran the ship aground; the bow stuck and remained immovable, but the stern was being broken up by the force of the waves. 42 The soldiers' plan was to kill the prisoners, so that none might swim away and escape; 43 but the centurion, wishing to save Paul, kept them from carrying out their plan. He ordered those who could swim to jump overboard first and make for the land, 44 and the rest to follow, some on planks and others on pieces of the ship. And so it was that all were brought safely to land.

Archipelago of Malta.

Understand the Word of God

This session will explore:

❖ Paul's skilful defence tactics

❖ the literary artistry and nautical technicalities of the adventure

❖ Paul's unexpected prophetic action to save the situation

Setting in the Book

Much has happened since the last passage we considered. Paul inflamed the crowds in the temple by his speech, and was taken into protective custody by the Romans (*Acts 22*). In an attempt to discover what the trouble was, the tribune arranged for Paul to appear before the chief priests in council. Paul cleverly set them at loggerheads with each other, Pharisees against Sadducees, by claiming that his only offence was to preach the Resurrection, knowing full well that the Sadducees did not believe in any resurrection of the dead (*23:6-10*). The Sadducees were infuriated and the Pharisees put on the defensive. That is the last we hear of any opposition to Paul from the Pharisees!

The tribune opted to send Paul to the governor at Caesarea. The Jews then planned to kidnap Paul on the journey, but the plot was leaked by Paul's nephew, acting as double-agent, and Paul was safely delivered (*23:16-22*). At Caesarea Paul was examined first by the governor, Felix (*Acts 24*). Despite having a Jewish wife, Felix felt quite unable to unravel the intricacies of this Jewish tangle and left Paul in custody at Caesarea when he demitted office at the end of his two-year tenure (*24:27*).

The new governor, Festus, was immediately briefed about Paul by the chief priests (Sadducees, of course), and summoned them to an examination of Paul. At this examination Paul was so frustrated that he exercised his rights as a Roman citizen by uncompromisingly appealing to Caesar (*25:11*). To Caesar, then, he must go.

Acts 25:11 Paul said: 'Now if I am in the wrong and have committed something for which I deserve to die, I am not trying to escape death; but if there is nothing to their charges against me, no one can turn me over to them. I appeal to the emperor.'

It may seem somewhat strange that Paul should appeal against an acquittal. Luke shows that Paul is vindicated by the Romans, and gives the reason for getting Paul to Rome, the end-point of the programme outlined in Acts 1:8. It is, however, also a clever move by Paul to release himself from the clutches of the chief priests. They will hardly follow him to Rome, and no Roman court would risk the entanglements of the Jewish Law.

After being paraded one last time by Festus before King Agrippa and Queen Berenice Paul makes yet another defence, which this time is generously larded with rhetorical ploys and classical allusions in honour of his royal audience. It is a masterpiece of Luke's art (*Acts 26*). Paul is now sent off to Rome.

Acts 28:7-9 Now in the neighbourhood of that place were lands belonging to the leading man of the island, named Publius, who received us and entertained us hospitably for three days. It so happened that the father of Publius lay sick in bed with fever and dysentery. Paul visited him and cured him by praying and putting his hands on him. After this happened, the rest of the people on the island who had diseases also came and were cured.

Once they have landed on Malta after the shipwreck, Paul continues his miraculous activity firstly by coming to no harm when he has been bitten by a poisonous snake (*28:3-6*). This fulfils Jesus' prophecy to his apostles, 'I have given you authority to tread on snakes and scorpions.' (*Luke 10:19*) Then he continues Jesus' healing mission by curing their host's father and other sick people on the island (*28:7-9*).

Shipwreck of the Minotaur, by William Turner.
The HMS Minotaur sank off the Netherlands in 1810 with great loss of life.

St Paul and the Viper, in St Anselm's Chapel, Canterbury Cathedral, UK.

What Kind of Text?

The story of Paul's shipwreck starts at the beginning of chapter 27 with a typical 'we-passage', where Luke gives details of travel arrangements, the route and the companions. The most important feature is that by the time they reached Cyprus, via the south coast of Turkey, it was already late September, so normally the closed season for shipping in the open sea. Navigational aids were so primitive that ancient ships tended to hug the shore where possible, which in turn brought into the equation danger from rocky coasts. In addition they were sailing westwards, so into the face of the prevailing trade-wind.

The excitement of this extended narrative speaks for itself. There is no doubt that Paul underwent shipwrecks of this kind. After all, he writes in 2 Corinthians 11:25: 'Three times I was shipwrecked; for a night and a day I was adrift at sea.' The author may have used a standard literary description to present the details of what actually happened.

In his later Commentary St Bede writes: In my earlier book, I said that the boat was a light craft made from osiers and covered with rough hides. But since then, looking through other books, I have discovered that such boats were hollowed out of a single tree-trunk, which the Greeks call monoxyles. Both these ideas probably tell us more about Northumbrian conditions in the eighth century than about Mediterranean shipping in the first. The earlier version suggests a coracle of the type known off the Northumbrian coast in the eighth century, but small clinker-built boats already existed in the Mediterranean area in the first century. A boat hollowed out from a single trunk would hardly be serviceable in a storm at sea.

Commentary: verse by verse reading

The Storm at Sea

Paul travels with the Augustan cohort (verse 1), which was an auxiliary detachment of Syrian troops stationed in Syria during much of the first century. Julius, the centurion in charge, obviously had to find his own transport for the prisoner and his entourage.

vv.9-12 The first part of the voyage was northwards up the eastern Mediterranean coast, and then westwards along the south coast of Turkey. At the port of Myra they embark on an Alexandrian ship bound for Italy, and come close to the island of Crete (*verses 5-7*).

In modern Jewish terminology 'the Fast' would mean the day commemorating the destruction of the temple. Since this had not yet occurred, it must be the Day of Atonement (*Leviticus 16:31*), which occurs in late September. There was still a reasonable chance of making Rome before the absolute end of the shipping season. Egypt was the bread-basket of Rome, and this late grain ship (see *verse 38*) from Alexandria would receive a tempting bonus.

vv.13-20 The conditions of the journey deteriorate rapidly. There exist ancient law court speeches in insurance cases, from which we may deduce the correct process to be followed during dire emergencies at sea. The process followed in this case is quite standard.

The first stage, indicated in verse 15, is to let go the sails and run before the wind. Verse 17 narrates that the ship is undergirded. This means that, using a small boat, a rope is run under the ship to hold the timbers together. To prevent excessive speeds and yawing they let out the sea anchor, for they are afraid of drifting towards the sandbanks of the Syrtis along the coast of North Africa.

St John Chysostom comments on the story: Again trials, again contrary winds. See how the life of the saint is so composed of all these things: he escaped the court, and they fall into a shipwreck and a storm. (Catena on the Acts of the Apostles 27.4-5)

They jettison the cargo to lighten the ship *(verse 18)*, which has probably taken water by now. They also jettison the ship's tackle *(verse 19)*. They are beginning to abandon hope *(verse 20)*.

vv.21-26 In an interruption to the 'we-passage', the prisoner Paul unexpectedly takes charge and acts as a prophet, calming the ship's crew, giving them sound advice and predicting a successful outcome. More precisely, he acts as a second Jonah. Jonah too was a passenger on a ship caught in a storm, and his advice to the ship's crew to pray and trust in God was what brought them through. Only Paul is not running away from God, so does not need to tell them to cast him overboard! Paul points out that, if they had in the first place listened to his prophetic advice (*verse 10*) that it was too late in the season to undertake this long journey across the open sea, they would not be in the mess in which they now find themselves.

Dramatic Arrival on Malta

vv.27-32 Suspecting that land is near, the sailors let out four sea anchors (*verse 29*).The selfishness of the ship's crew, who try to escape in a boat, provides a little subsidiary drama illustrating Paul's confidence. Casting off the lifeboat is a serious step.

vv.33-38 The 'we-passage' is interrupted again. Paul once again encourages those on board with the definite hope of survival. The reference to taking bread and giving thanks, breaking it and eating is not sufficiently detailed to suggest a Eucharist in the full sense of commemorating the Lord's Supper. It is a eucharist in the sense of a thanksgiving to God. Finally, they jettison even their food-supplies to lessen the draught as they seem to be rapidly approaching some shore.

vv.39-44 The island turns out to be Malta (*28:1*). A sandy bay on the north-east coast is traditionally known as St Paul's Bay. In the dramatic final stages of the story the ship runs aground and breaks up. Julius commands that the prisoners should not be killed. Some swimming, others clinging to planks, they are all brought safely ashore to experience the kindness of the natives (*28:2*).

Jonah says to the men on board: Pick me up and throw me into the sea; then the sea will quiet down for you; for I know it is because of me that this great storm has come upon you. (Jonah 1:12)

The Venerable Bede comments on the shipwreck: This ship perished because it did not glide over the waves with a smooth movement. Rather it became violently stuck on the sea floor, part held fast, while part was broken up by the smashing waves. Such, without a doubt, is the fate of a mind attached to this world. When such a one has made no effort to trample mundane desires underfoot, he fixes the prow of his intention radically upon the earth, and therefore with the waves of cares he dashes to pieces the whole structure of works that follow. (Commentary on Acts, c. 27)

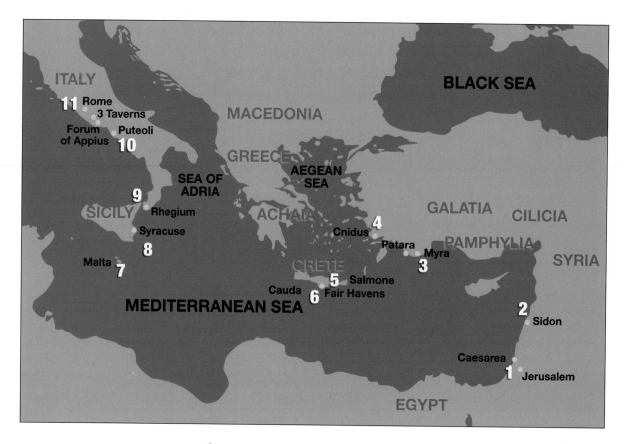

St Paul's journey to Rome.

The Word Lives On

Not surprisingly, the length of the story of the shipwreck has defied any attempt to include it in the readings for the liturgy. It has, however, frequently been dramatically represented in art.

Live the Word of God

Listen again to the reading: Acts 27:9-44

Suggestions for reflection and prayer

If you are caught in a desperate situation what is your reaction?

❖ Do you panic, persevere or pray?

❖ What is the correct combination?

❖ Should we expect panic-prayers to be answered?

❖ Does God answer prayers at all?

Paul was obviously preserved for a reason.

❖ At this stage of reading the Acts of the Apostles, what would you say was Paul's most important achievement?

❖ Have you ever read one of his letters right through? Try one, a chapter a day!

One often hears of people saved from a crash by the sheer chance of missing the bus/train/plane.

❖ Is there such a thing as chance, or does God arrange every detail?

❖ Does God take better care of some people than of others?

❖ Do vast natural disasters shake your faith? Why not?

Is natural evil in any way the same as moral evil? Should we use the same word in both cases?

St Bede the Venerable comments: A most beautiful allegorical sense is evident in this passage. No one escapes the tempests of this world except those who are nourished by the bread of life. One who in the night of present tribulations depends for all strength on wisdom, fortitude, temperance and justice will soon, with the shining forth of divine help, reach the port of salvation which he had sought. (Commentary on Acts, c.27)

Saint Paul on Malta, by Adam Elsheimer.

Paul in Rome

Hear the Word of God

Read Acts 28:15-31

15 The believers from there, when they heard of us, came as far as the Forum of Appius and Three Taverns to meet us. On seeing them, Paul thanked God and took courage. 16 When we came into Rome, Paul was allowed to live by himself, with the soldier who was guarding him.

17 Three days later he called together the local leaders of the Jews. When they had assembled, he said to them, 'Brothers, though I had done nothing against our people or the customs of our ancestors, yet I was arrested in Jerusalem and handed over to the Romans. 18 When they had examined me, the Romans wanted to release me, because there was no reason for the death penalty in my case. 19 But when the Jews objected, I was compelled to appeal to the emperor—even though I had no charge to bring against my nation. 20 For this reason therefore I have asked to see you and speak with you, since it is for the sake of the hope of Israel that I am bound with this chain.' 21 They replied, 'We have received no letters from Judea about you, and none of the brothers coming here has reported or spoken anything evil about you. 22 But we would like to hear from you what you think, for with regard to this sect we know that everywhere it is spoken against.'

23 After they had fixed a day to meet him, they came to him at his lodgings in great numbers. From morning until evening he explained the matter to them, testifying to the kingdom of God and trying to convince them about Jesus both from the law of Moses and from the prophets. 24 Some were convinced by what he had said, while others refused to believe. 25 So they disagreed with each other; and as they were leaving, Paul made one further statement: 'The Holy Spirit was right in saying to your ancestors through the prophet Isaiah,

26 "Go to this people and say,
You will indeed listen, but never understand,
and you will indeed look, but never perceive.

27 For this people's heart has grown dull,
  and their ears are hard of hearing,
  and they have shut their eyes;
  so that they might not look with their eyes,

Opposite: The Apostles St Peter and St Paul, by El Greco.

and listen with their ears,

and understand with their heart and turn—

and I would heal them."

28 Let it be known to you then that this salvation of God has been sent to the Gentiles; they will listen.'

30 He lived there for two whole years at his own expense and welcomed all who came to him, 31 proclaiming the kingdom of God and teaching about the Lord Jesus Christ with all boldness and without hindrance.

San Paolo fuori le Mura, Rome. (St Paul Outside the Walls, Rome)

Understand the Word of God

Setting in the Book

This final chapter of the book introduces us to the Church at Rome, but only barely. It is concerned mostly with Paul's relationship with the Jewish community of Rome. A brief look at the city of Rome at this time, and at the Christian community in Rome will be helpful, before we consider why the Acts of the Apostles ends in this manner.

Rome was the centre of the world, in a way in which no other city has ever been. It dominated the world around the Mediterranean Sea, spreading out its tentacles to Ethiopia in the South and Britain in the North, Spain in the West and India in the East, sucking in goods from even further afield.

Cicero tells us that not a penny changed hands in Gaul without being entered on Roman ledgers. The animal population of North Africa has never recovered from the depradations of the capture of wild beasts for the amusement of the Roman masses in watching their slaughter at the Games. Vast tracts of the East were so heavily chained by debt to individual Roman senators that they were in effect their private domains. At the same time the attraction of Rome was such that Romans complained that the Orontes, a river in Syria, flowed into the Tiber: peoples, gods and customs from every nation could be encountered, prospering, in the streets of Rome. The rich enjoyed splendid mansions on the seven hills of Rome, while the poor jostled among the tenement-blocks of marshy and fever-ridden Trastevere.

The Book of Revelation, which represents Rome as the great prostitute, lists the worldwide flow of imports:

...gold, silver, jewels and pearls, fine linen, purple, silk and scarlet, all kinds of scented wood, all articles of ivory, all articles of costly wood, bronze, iron and marble, cinnamon, spice, incense, myrrh, frankincense, wine, olive oil, choice flour and wheat, cattle and sheep, horses and chariots, slaves - and human lives (Revelation 18:12-13).

Saint Paul the Apostle,
by Marco Pino.

The foundation of the Christian community in Rome is shrouded in mystery. So is its relationship to this visit of Paul to Rome. The Roman historian Suetonius reports that there were Christians in Rome in 49AD. In Romans 16:10 greetings are sent to the household of Aristobulus, and it is tempting to think that the first Christians in Rome could have been slaves brought by Aristobulus, grandson of King Herod, who died in Rome in the late 40s.

Tradition regards Peter as the founder of the Church at Rome, but when can this have been? It is scarcely credible that Peter had already been in Rome when Paul wrote to the Romans in the mid-50s, for Paul would surely have mentioned him. Romans 16:5-15 presents several different house churches, but there is no sign of any central organization, which could fit the idea that Peter was its presiding elder, the official referred to in 1 Timothy 3:1. The notion that Peter was bishop of Rome is, of course, anachronistic, for it is not until the second century that the office of bishop as such begins to come into focus.

Romans 15:23-24 But now, with no further place for me in these regions, I desire, as I have for many years, to come to you when I go to Spain. For I do hope to see you on my journey and to be sent on by you, once I have enjoyed your company for a little while.

When he wrote to the Romans, Paul was planning a mission to Spain and hoped that the Romans would back him up (*Romans 15:23-24*). Luke, who makes no mention of Paul's letters, gives no hint of this plan either. Such a plan would scarcely fit realistically into Paul's schedule as outlined in Acts. When Paul is brought under guard to Rome a Christian community clearly exists, and yet the dialogue between Paul and the Jews there suggests that this is the first encounter of the Roman Jews with Christian beliefs.

What Kind of Text?

The ending of Acts has often been regarded as an unsolved puzzle. Why does Luke stop here? What happened to Paul afterwards? In fact it makes perfect sense. Luke's purpose is not to give a picture of the Roman community, nor even of Paul's activity there. If he were writing a history of Paul's missionary activity it would be intolerably clumsy to end in midstream with this two-year stay in Rome and no indication of what happened afterwards. We are not even told whether he was eventually brought to trial.

Luke's purpose is in fact to bring to a conclusion the grand plan of Acts, announced in 1:8, of bringing the message of the Good News 'in Jerusalem, in all Judea and Samaria, and to the ends of the earth'. This last expression is, in Jewish literature, a cipher for Rome, and here the plan is accomplished through Paul's agency. On various occasions also we have seen that Luke is anxious to show that there is no hostility between Christianity and Rome. This is strongly reinforced by the picture of Paul barely restricted in his movements from beginning to end of his stay at Rome. His presence in Rome is a convenience rather than a constriction.

From the beginning of the Gospel of Luke the author has been concerned with the question of theodicy: Christianity is the completion of Judaism, the fulfilment of the promises to Abraham and of the careful preparation of the people of Israel down the ages. Yet the Jews rejected the message and the Gentiles embraced it. The pattern seen in the Gospel reaches its completion in Acts. The first chapters show a minimal response from Israel and the formation of an ideal community at Jerusalem. All this comes to an end with the martyrdom of Stephen. In his final speech Stephen reads the rejection of the message by Judaism as the fulfilment of their disobedience throughout history and a preparation for their refusal of the Good News. On two occasions, once in Asia Minor (13:46) and once in Greece (18:6), Paul has been rejected by the Jews, and has formally and biblically noted that he has no alternative but to turn to the Gentiles. Here in Rome he completes the pattern with the third and most solemn declaration of all. This is the historical lesson presented by Paul's activity in Rome.

By Jesus' manifesto in the synagogue at Nazareth (Luke 4:16-30) Luke shows that Jesus intends the message for the Gentiles. In the parable of the great feast (Luke 14:15-24) the refusal of the original guests to attend compels the host to summon first the poor, the crippled, the blind and the lame, and then to go outside the city to the open roads and the hedgerows. This is clearly an allegory of Jesus' welcome for sinners, tax-collectors and prostitutes within Judaism, followed by his welcome for the Gentiles.

From St John Chrysostom: Observe, if you please, how Paul himself was affected in a human way. "On seeing them," it says, "he took courage." In spite of all the miracles he had worked, the sight of the brothers still afforded him assistance. From this we learn that he received comfort and its opposite as other people do. (Homilies on the Acts of the Apostles 54)

Christian curiosity inevitably asks what happened to Paul after this. Was he brought to trial? Was he acquitted? Did he ever get to Spain? How was he brought back to Rome for his martyrdom, traditionally a beheading at St Paul's outside the Walls? Eusebius of Caesarea, that very solid fourth-century Christian historian, deduces from 2 Timothy 4 that Paul was imprisoned and tried a second time at Rome, and was expecting to be executed (verse 6). Many, but not all, modern scholars regard this data as questionable, holding that the letter was not written personally by Paul. No certainty is possible, except that Acts is brought by Luke to a due and satisfactory conclusion.

Commentary: verse by verse reading

The arrival in Rome

vv.15-16 The last two paragraphs of this final 'we-passage' are typical, careful notes on the progress of Paul's travel. The Forum of Appius and the Three Taverns are both stages on the Via Appia, the great Roman road entering Rome from the south, respectively about seventy and fifty-five kilometres from the walls of Rome. When Paul arrives in Rome his accommodation was, as we have already remarked, more a convenience than a constriction. There were no legal arrangements for long-term imprisonment. Sentences were sharp and swift and did not include lengthy periods of imprisonment, for which no provision was made. Senatorial prisoners could be kept in the custody of their trusted peers, but there is no question of that here, and an informal arrangement has to be put in place.

vv.17-22 The first meeting with the Jewish leaders is devoted to showing that there was no incompatibility between Paul's message and Judaism, and above all that there is no hostility between Paul and Rome. It was only the groundless objection of the Jews which had switched into action the Roman mechanism that defended Paul from their murderous intentions. The Jewish leaders are compelled to agree that they have nothing adverse to report about Paul (*verse 21*).

Opposite: Via Appia and the Three Taverns.

Acceptance and rejection

vv.23-28 The final scene completes the message of the book. Paul argues for Christ from the Scriptures, just as the Risen Christ himself had done on the road to Emmaus (*Luke 24:27*). As throughout Acts, some are convinced, but the rest are incoherently hostile.

Finally, Paul makes the solemn declaration from Isaiah, explaining their refusal in scriptural terms. This is the text used also in the parable chapter of the synoptic gospels (*Mark 4:12, Matthew 13:14-15, Luke 8:10*) to explain the failure of the Jews to accept the message of Jesus, and in John 12:40 at the conclusion of Jesus' ministry. It must have been one of the commonplaces of the early Christian community: the inexplicable failure of the Jews to accept the message was foretold in Scripture. It was necessary that it should be so.

vv.29-31 The final verses of the Acts of the Apostles stress once again the complete freedom of Paul, who both proclaims the kingdom of God and teaches about the Lord Jesus Christ 'with all boldness (Greek *parresia*) and without hindrance'.

St John Chrysostom comments: Look, again it is not by miracles but with the law and the prophets that he silences them, and this is what he does on every occasion. And yet Paul had the power to perform miracles, but then it would no longer be a matter of faith. For this was a great miracle, to discourse from the law and the prophets. (Homilies on the Acts of the Apostles 55)

Mark 4:11-12 Jesus said: To you has been given the secret of the kingdom of God, but for those outside, everything comes in parables; in order that "they may indeed look, but not perceive, and may indeed listen, but not understand; so that they may not turn again and be forgiven."

To 'speak with boldness' is characteristic of Paul as portrayed in Acts. Further examples are given below:

9:28 Paul went in and out among them in Jerusalem, speaking boldly in the name of the Lord.

13:46 Then both Paul and Barnabas spoke out boldly.

14:3 They remained for a long time, speaking boldly for the Lord.

18:26 He began to speak boldly in the synagogue.

19:8 He entered the synagogue and for three months spoke out boldly, and argued persuasively about the kingdom of God.

The Word Lives On

The passage about Paul's final stay in Rome and the conclusion of the Acts is read, omitting the final confrontation with the Jews, on the final Saturday of Eastertide, to conclude the history of the early Church. It is read also on the Feast of the Dedication of the Lateran Basilica, the mother-church of Rome and the Pope's own Cathedral (November 18th).

St Paul, statue in front of St Peter's Basilica.

Live the Word of God

Listen again to the reading: Acts 28:15-31

Suggestions for reflection and prayer

The conclusion of Acts with the arrival of Paul in Rome stresses the function of that city as focus of unity in the Church.

❖ What does the centrality of Rome contribute to the Church?

❖ How could I work to achieve the recognition of this by other Christians?

❖ Is my own loyalty to the teaching office of the Bishop of Rome sufficiently strong?

❖ Do I take the trouble to inform myself about important papal teaching and the teaching of my own bishop?

Since the time of the writing of Acts the notion of 'the ends of the earth' has considerably expanded, and Christianity has truly spread to all nations.

❖ This is grounds for great rejoicing and thanksgiving.

❖ Christianity in the developing nations is often more spontaneous, fervent and joyful than in more developed countries. What can I learn from such Christians?

❖ Christians in the developing nations are also my brothers and sisters. Can I and should I do more to help them?

Prisoners need the prayers of the Church, especially those imprisoned for long periods, those imprisoned wrongfully and for their fidelity to their consciences.

❖ Pray for prisoners suffering for their Christian faith.

❖ Pray for the release of those wrongfully imprisoned.

❖ Pray that the conduct of prisons be aimed at the good of the prisoners.

❖ Pray for those charged with the care of prisons and prisoners.

St John Chysostom writes: Rome received Paul in chains and saw him crowned. He added trophies to trophies, invincible as he was. Corinth held him for two years, Asia for three, and this city for two. Then for a second time he enters this city, when he has reached perfection. Thus he escaped and, having filled the whole world, brought his life to a close. (Homilies on the Acts, 55).

Picture Credits